*Majken*

by
**Carl Lawrence**

THOMAS NELSON PUBLISHERS
Nashville

AUG     1981

Unless otherwise noted, Bible quotations are from the King James
Version of the Bible.

*Copyright © 1981 by Haven of Rest*

**Library of Congress Cataloging in Publication Data**

Lawrence, Carl.
  Majken.
    1. Church work with children.   2. Broby, Majken.
3. Mission Kinderheim.   I. Title.
BV639.C4L3        259'.22       81-291
ISBN 0-8407-5762-X       AACR1

To those who have quietly prayed, "Lord, what will You have me to do?" and then have done it; and whose names are recorded in the Book that will never go out of print, this book is gratefully dedicated.

# CONTENTS

# 1

# LEARNING
# TO WALK

The confusion and noise that accompanies a ship's preparation for a long ocean voyage was lost to Majken Broby as she slowly made her way across the deck. She stepped over a coil of rope and took hold of the upper bar of the railing. Her eyes never left the gangplank. Involuntarily she reached up and tightened the collar of the new red wool suit purchased just for this occasion. The chill August breeze that gave the first hint of another Swedish winter swept across her face. In doing so, it dried her few remaining tears and renewed her spirit.

She pressed her frail body against the rail. Her left leg throbbed just enough to remind her that her leg was not yet fully restored. The breeze blew a little of her brown hair into her eyes. She reached up with her gloved hand and pushed the lock of hair back under her pillbox hat.

Her eyes continued to move down the gangplank, following the elderly couple as they helped each other make their way back to the dock.

During her thirty years of life, Majken had never been far from her mother and father. Her arms trembled slightly as she watched them take that last step onto the dock. She realized that in a few moments the whistle would blow, a boatswain would shout a few orders, the ropes would drop into the water, and Majken Broby would be on her way to America. It was a moment she had waited for, prayed for, and worked for. Now that it had arrived, she received it almost as an intruder.

There was never really any doubt in the Broby family that there would come a day when one of the children would leave for the mission field. For years their home had been the center of the mission activity of the church. No matter how low the food supply might be, Gustav and Sigrid Broby always issued an invitation to any visiting missionary to sit around their table. Now, Majken's two older brothers had other vocations. Her older sister was dead from diphtheria, and Majken stood aboard a ship knowing only one thing for certain. She was leaving home and going to America. But was she a missionary?

It was a journey that had begun when she was four years old. Anxiously Gustav and Sigrid had stood at her bedside as the doctor told them to pray for the best but prepare for the worst. Diphtheria was considered a plague. But little Majken was unaware of the danger. Though bathed in sweat, weak from not being able to take nourishment, her eager young mind concentrated on the day she would be a nurse. "I will help people get well and tell them about Jesus at the same time." It seemed so simple to a four-year-old child.

Faced with the precariousness of her daughter's existence, Sigrid Broby knelt down and gave Majken to the Lord. It was not a bargaining session. The Broby family were too mature in their prayer life to do something like that. Rather, Sigrid voiced her simple acceptance of the very real fact that Jesus Christ was not only Savior, but Master of their lives as individuals and as a family. "She is Yours, Father," she prayed. "If You want to take her home, she is Yours. If You want her to live, that too must be according to Your will. But I promise You this, Lord. If You leave her with us, I will never stand in her way if she wants to leave us to serve You."

The doctor was wrong. Majken did recover, and in a short time, she was nursing her homemade dolls and telling them about Jesus.

She never lost her childhood dream. When chemistry formulas seemed impossible to memorize, when her back ached too much to make another bed, when she struggled to empty another bedpan without becoming ill, she reminded herself of the day when she would be a graduate nurse.

Not only did she become a nurse, she went on to graduate school and became an X-ray specialist. Steadily she acquired more responsibility, until she was supervisor and chief X-ray technician for a three-hundred-bed hospital in Varberg.

As much as she enjoyed her career, there was a void in her life. She knew that there was much more to life than what she had experienced. *Someday,* she thought, *that will be taken care of when I settle down, marry, and raise a family.* She dreamed of the day when she would take her own child over to visit "Grandma."

She was not unhappy, but she was not content. *I'm happy,* she thought, *but I want to be joyful.*

Some days she was just too tired to think about it. It was on such a day that she unlocked the door to her private quarters in the hospital and fell into her scarred, comfortable easy chair.

Letting out a sigh, a private signal that she was glad that another day was over, she reached up and untied the string under her chin. Her small, starched cap fell to the floor. She would pick it up later. Just now she was too exhausted. Today she had X-rayed more than her share of refugees—frightened men, women, and children who were arriving in Sweden in hordes, trying to escape the aftermath of Hitler.

13

Especially disturbing was the number of refugees who had the mysterious severe headaches. Several times the nurses discussed this strange malady, but never with any conclusions, and finally even Majken began to think of them as routine.

She leaned back in her chair, dropped her arms to her sides, and kicked off her shoes. The back of her head felt heavy, and she began to rotate her head to ease the tension. She stopped when what felt like a little jolt of electricity shot up the back of her head; then she concentrated on wiggling her toes, reviving her circulation after standing on her feet for nine hours.

The familiar feeling of loneliness and unfulfillment began to creep into her mind. She refused to accept it, and as she had done many times before, she slipped to her knees in front of her chair. She buried both elbows in the frayed cushion and cradled her head in her hands. Then as the strange feeling of what she termed "nothingness" crept over her, she began to give words to her prayer. At first it was a simple statement; but the urgency grew, and soon her petition was accentuated with tears.

"Lord, just knowing You is not enough. I must know what Your calling is for my life. Lord, I feel like I don't really belong . . . I feel like a stranger going through the motions of being a person. Lord . . ." She paused and searched for the right word to express herself. "Lord, I feel like a refugee. . . ." She nodded her head in agreement. "Yes, Lord, I feel like a refugee. . . ." Her voice took on a new timbre as she pressed her elbows into the cushion. "Lord, that's what I am, a refugee. . . ." Her voice broke, and her shoulders shook with sobs. She wept deeply and then cried out, "Lord, I'm tired of being a refugee. I want to be a pilgrim . . . a pilgrim . . . not a refugee . . . a pilgrim. . . ."

The words trailed off into silence. Her shoulders became still. In her mind's eye a picture began to come into focus. There it was in front of her: a wide street. It was wider than any street she had known in Sweden. It stretched off end-lessly into the distance. Coming down the street were peo-ple. There were all kinds of people, all colors, wearing different kinds of clothing. In front of the adults were in-numerable children. They were walking toward Majken, and they all were wringing their hands in despair, staring at Majken through hollowed-out eyes. Their eyes told of im-measurable suffering and hardship—even the children's. They looked so old. They all wore ragged clothes, and they kept coming. There seemed to be no end to the procession.

"No, no, Lord. I can't help them," she cried out as she raised her head. The intensity of her protest surprised her. She dropped her head back into her hands and repeated in a soft but firm tone, "I can't help them." Then she heard the words: *The power of the Cross . . . the power of the Cross . . . the power of the Cross.*

She was startled. It was as if someone had stood by her side repeating the words. Still on her knees, she looked around the room. The furniture was the same, old and worn; the bed was still neatly made; three clean uniforms hung in the half-open closet across the room. She was alone.

Majken stood up. This was no dream. She knew in her heart that in some mysterious way she was changed. She sat on the edge of the bed, stared out the window, and began to think about the wide street, the wringing hands, the haunted eyes.

It was a vision that she carried with her to the evening meal, to her bed that night, into the X-ray room the next morning. She told no one of her experience, but she thought about it constantly. Her interest in her patients changed. She no longer X-rayed numbers; they were peo-ple. Always she looked at their hands and then at their eyes.

She was especially drawn to those with the mysterious headaches.

For several weeks this continued. The number of ref-

15

ugees increased as her personal distaste for Germany grew. She blamed that country alone for all the misery which passed through the hospital. These were the tragic victims of a senseless war, scarred for life by the Third Reich. She was certain of one thing—she would go anywhere in the world to work except Germany.

Then one day there was another flash of light, but this was no vision. Before she could regain control, a terrible pain shot up her back and into her head, violently knocking her into unconsciousness.

She awoke to a scene in which she had participated hundreds of times as a nurse—only now, she was the patient. Excruciating pain racked her head and left side. A doctor left the room carrying a long syringe. She knew what it had been used for. They had just completed a spinal tap. The nurse followed him out.

She tried to raise her head, but it ached too much. *They are doing this to me*, she told herself. *I'm not sick. They are wrong. I'll show them.* She attempted to get out of bed and realized with a gasp that her entire left side was paralyzed. Her head fell back on her pillow. Perspiration ran down her forehead. Her body felt icy cold. "Oh, no!" she cried in desperation. The tears ran down her face and soaked the pillow. "I am a cripple! I am crippled. . . ." Her words trailed off as the medication lulled her into merciful sleep.

The doctors called it encephalitis; the X-ray technicians dubbed it "the refugee headache"; her parents were told it was "inflammation of the brain," but Majken called it "brain fever." The doctors knew no more about the treatment than they knew about the cause.

"Majken," said the chief surgeon, "you may never walk again, but you will be able to get around in a wheelchair. We will give you the best of therapy, but right now, I want you to rest. You need time to heal."

The numbness left her mind but not her left side. Panic

16

alternated with pain, dominating the minutes, the hours, the weeks. All of her self-confidence, her self-sufficiency, her superb training were now locked away in a body racked with pain, self-doubt, and no small amount of self-pity.

"But what about the vision?" she would ask, staring up at the ceiling.

The words of the doctor came back to her. "Majken, you need time to heal." She learned to live with pain. At first she thought only of her left leg, now merely a marble-colored piece of flesh attached to her body. There was no healing there. Then gradually she began to wonder if maybe there wasn't another kind of healing needed. The thought persisted for several weeks.

One day, the therapy had been especially grueling. It all seemed so hopeless; yet surprisingly, as she was returned to her room, she felt peaceful. She began to pray:

> Dear Lord, I was wondering what it was like to be one of them, those who were so helpless, those that I felt so proud that I could help, those that I would talk to and try to encourage. Oh, Lord, there were even times when I would say to myself, "Lord, I am glad that I am not like them." You remember that, don't You, Lord?
>
> Well, Father, now I am one of them. I am helpless, with people waiting on me. Just as they have been driven by an enemy from their country and their homes, losing everything, now, I too have been driven from that which I had put my trust in. Lord, here I am. What is next for me?

The tears flowed, cleansing the soul of its final vestiges of resentment and self-pity. "Lord, I know that I am not fit to be a pilgrim until I have been a refugee."

The pain remained, but Majken knew that the healing had begun. It was a private celebration of thanksgiving each time she was lifted into the hydrotherapy tank; each time she winced with pain as her legs and arms were massaged.

Even the nights became more bearable, and she concentrated on moving her paralyzed leg. It was a performance that never had a proper audience, until one day the therapist gasped in surprise. The leg had moved.

The next celebration came when she lifted her left arm. Slowly, with excruciating pain, one inch became two, and then three. Slowly, painfully, the healing continued. She graduated to crutches, and then there was only one crutch. Her reward was a half-day job preparing medicine in the hospital.

Christmas was a special time. Not only would she be going home for three weeks without therapy, but the doctors told her they had a special present for her.

The day before Christmas, she worked her way to the X-ray room with the help of her trusty crutch. It was the first time she had been back since she collapsed twenty-one months earlier. She walked in to the cheers of her colleagues. Above her X-ray machine hung a sign, "Welcome Back to X-Ray"; below was a special chair designed so that she could sit and run the machine. She was officially back to work.

There were other encouragements as well. Her favorite cousin, Joseph Mattson-Boze, and his wife, Daga, had moved to America to a place called Chicago. They had asked Majken to visit them, if and when she was well enough. She had talked to her father about the invitation many times, and he had always encouraged her, certain that the day of her full recovery would never come.

Instead, several months later she declared that she was well enough to go.

"Majken," Gustav protested, "do you think they would build you a special chair for the X-ray machine in America? No, Majken, I think not. America is the land of the healthy." He patted her shoulder sympathetically, but Majken could see that his resistance was fading.

"Father, if America is the land of the healthy, then soon I

will throw this crutch away, and I will swim to America.''
Though she said it with a broad smile, her father knew her
well enough to know that she was determined.

Five months later, Majken opened the door to her quarters at the hospital for the last time. Leaning against the wall
were her crutches. Slowly she walked across the room and
placed her cane between them. She left the room un-
assisted, a noticeable limp the only physical reminder of her
past ordeal.

The deafening sound of the ship's whistle startled her out
of her reverie. She realized she was waving automatically to
her parents on the dock, which quickly receded as the ship
moved into the harbor. Soon she had to strain her eyes to
see the two forms at all. She dropped her arm to her side
and turned to walk to her cabin. Her leg ached from the
morning's activities, but there was no trace of a limp. Taking a deep breath of fresh air, she said aloud, ''Lord, thank
You for making this refugee a pilgrim.''

# 2

# ONE STEP
# AT A TIME

The agent who had sold Majken the ticket to America had assured her that the ship would "glide" across the Atlantic. It didn't. It creaked, moaned, lurched, and seemed to search out the largest waves to crash into. It threw buckets of salt water at whoever ventured out on the deck for fresh air.

Fortunately, Majken had a large supply of medicine for seasickness and a book on how to learn the English language in two weeks. She voraciously devoured both during the ten-day voyage and was not saddened when the Captain announced their last night at sea. They would reach New York harbor early the next day.

Majken spent the evening feverishly rehearsing some of the more important sentences that she had learned, like "How do you do?"; "Nice to meet you"; "Where is the powder room?" and other phrases that the book said everyone in America used. She concentrated on speaking slowly and distinctly, a practice she would discover drew rather blank stares from her listeners.

It was just as well that she was unaware of that problem. For the first time since her illness she became apprehensive, not only about her arrival but about her future. What was it God wanted her to do in America? Would there be any of those wringing hands, hollow eyes, and wide streets in Chicago? Was this to be another training school like her hospital bed? If so, what would this course be like? And how long would it last?

She narrowed her thoughts to the more immediate problem of what would happen if no one met her in New York. She did not speak the language. She didn't even know where Chicago lay in relation to New York. Her finances were limited to the last Swedish krona she had taken out of her savings before she left.

She sat on the side of her bunk and unfolded the letter from Cousin Joseph, already limp and worn from much rereading. She checked the list of things he told her to do when she arrived in New York and confirmed in her mind that she knew them all.

She had sent a letter to Joseph's friend in New York and had given him the name of the ship, its arrival date, a recent picture of herself, and a description in great detail of what she would be wearing: the red wool suit, the pillbox hat, and long gloves.

Convinced that everything was in order, she lay back and attempted to go to sleep.

She woke up tossing in bed. At first she thought it was the motion of the ship and then realized that for the first time the ship was indeed gliding; it was she who was tossing and turning. She could hear people moving about outside her door. Too nervous to eat breakfast, she dressed quickly and made her way to the deck. She joined the other passengers who were lining the rail. Each was pointing to the New York skyline.

The crowd on deck grew quiet. With only the sound of the engines and a few sea gulls, the ship passed the Statue of Liberty. Majken stood and gazed in awe, mesmerized not so much by the size of the figure, but rather by what it represented. The harbor itself did not garner such respect.

People began to crush against the rail as the engines stopped and several tugboats came alongside to guide the ship. The immigration and customs officials already had boarded and arrival formalities were completed.

Majken was afraid that she might lose her hat in the press of the crowd. She tolerated the confusion good-naturedly, hoping that when she got ashore the people in America would have more respect and there wouldn't be all this shoving, uproarious laughing, and boisterousness. The sun beamed strongly, as the ship was pushed closer to the dock. Perspiration began to run down Majken's face. At first she tried to blot it off with her gloved hands, but they soon were sodden, and she took a handkerchief from her purse. She was learning one of her first lessons about America. August in New York is not the same as August in Sweden.

A loud shout went up as the gangplank went down. People anxiously called and waved from the dock. Some carried signs with people's names on them. She was swept along by the surging crowd of passengers as they headed for the arms of their loved ones.

Clutching a small overnight bag in one hand and her soggy handkerchief in the other, she took her first step onto American soil. Now all she had to do was collect her luggage and find Cousin Joseph's friend.

She looked in every direction, but her view was blocked by the crowds of people embracing all around her. For a moment she was sure that she was going to faint. How would the man who was to meet her ever find her in this crowd? She wanted to take her hat off, but she had described it in such detail in her letter that she was certain Joseph's friend would be looking for it. Her long gloves, now soiled and grimy, were heavy in the heat, but she dared not remove them either.

Suddenly she felt someone staring at her. She turned a little and looked out of the corner of her eye. Standing a few feet away was an older man, blonde and fresh-faced, with a photograph in his hand. He peered at a letter in his other hand, and then he looked at Majken. If she had any inhibitions about talking to strange men, she brushed them aside. She walked over, pulled off a soggy glove, extended her hand, and spoke politely in English. "I am Majken Broby. I welcome to New York."

The trip by taxi to Grand Central Station was marked by exclamations of surprise from Majken at how tall the buildings were, how crowded the streets were, and how thinly dressed the ladies were.

After buying her ticket to Chicago and checking her trunk, Majken was taken to a hotel. Her escort bade a cordial farewell, and she went to her room.

She spent much of her first night in America in prayer, her red wool suit draped over a chair in the stifling heat of her room. She thanked God for a safe arrival and that she had been met. She thought how terrible it must be to arrive somewhere unexpected, unnoticed, uncared for, and in many cases unwanted.

The next morning she was amazed at how quickly she adapted to her new environment. It was not difficult to enter into the spirit of the push and shove of the crowd in the train station. With the help of a porter she found her train and a comfortable seat by the window. Once out of New York City, the landscape changed into small towns and countryside. She watched the scenery with pleasure for several hours, then practiced the English she had learned on board ship.

Finally, after a long journey, the conductor announced "Chicago."

Again, she moved with the crowd to the door. This time there was no apprehension. She knew that Joseph and Daga would be there.

Through the clamor on the platform Majken heard, sweet

23

and distinct as a melody from a symphony, *"Volkommen till Amerika, Majken*—Welcome to America, Majken."

Joyously she fell into the outstretched arms of her cousins. She had taken another major step towards where God would have her be.

# 3

# CHICAGO

In a few days, Chicago and Majken were old friends. She especially liked the cool breeze that blew across Lake Michigan. It reminded her of home. There was only one uniquely American habit that she knew she could never adopt. She watched with considerable fascination, mingled with equal parts of disgust and consternation, as people took a small packet out of their pocket and unwrapped it. Then they did two things that her organized mind could not comprehend. They threw the wrapper on the ground, and stuck what appeared to be a piece of candy-flavored wax in their mouth and chewed vigorously. At first she watched and waited for them to swallow, but they never did.

Within a month she had seen most of the city and felt that her days as a tourist must end. She sat down in Cousin Joseph's living room with pencil and paper to take stock of her life.

There were several priorities. First, she must learn English. Second, she must get a job. She could not be a parasite and let her cousins support her, although they would never have viewed it from that perspective.

She locked herself away in her room for two weeks, vigorously studying the language. Then she enrolled in an evening English class at a local university. In a week's time she had a job as a nurse's assistant at Swedish Covenant Hospital. She found that many of the people working there were of Swedish descent, which facilitated her work but allowed her to practice English at the same time.

Her new job added another priority to her list. The requirements to be a registered nurse were quite different in the United States from what they were in Sweden. The studies did not seem to be any more stringent, but the emphasis was different. After some investigation, she found a nursing school two hours' ride from Cousin Joseph's house. She calculated that four hours a day would be precious time wasted, so she located a small apartment which was in close proximity to her English classes, the hospital, and the nursing school. She would study language three nights a week, work five days a week, and devote the rest of her time to her nursing degree. Saturdays were free to study, and Sundays for church and visiting with Joseph and Daga.

After several months of this schedule, she began to realize that her English was in some cases better than her teachers', who often spoke with a decided accent. She dropped the language classes and concentrated on her nurses' training and her job. But through it all she was acutely aware that this was only a bend in the road, a time of preparation for something much bigger.

It was not long before her patients at the hospital began to ask for her when they were to be sent home. She decided to take up private nursing, which was much less demanding and left her more time for personal study. She spent hours at the public libraries, poring over atlases and periodicals, reading what was happening in Europe and Asia. She felt drawn to pictures of refugees, which seemed always to find their way to the front pages of the Chicago *Tribune* and other major newspapers. Her interest never faltered. She knew that when she saw the outstretched hands and hollow eyes of her vision she would recognize them and be ready to respond.

For two years she worked, studied, prayed, and grew. Her English now was fluent. She found it simple to rattle off colloquialisms and never tired of learning new words. Then, on February 1, 1950, she read aloud some of the most beautiful words she had seen since arriving in America. It was a very official-looking document she showed to her cousins, with a gold seal and her name printed in old English script: Majken Broby, Registered Nurse. It was signed in Chicago, Illinois. Now she could wear her cap again.

She continued her private nursing and found that along the way she was learning another very important lesson: how to handle money. She had always been frugal, and she had never been selfish, but now the Lord taught her how truly to give to help those in need. She never ceased to marvel at how far her meager paycheck went when she dedicated it to Him and waited for His direction in spending. She never wanted for anything materially, physically, or spiritually. These were good days.

There was another unexpected event which brought the final phase of her "training." She had been working, saving, and studying for three years when Joseph and Daga convinced her that she needed a vacation. Everyone in America took vacations, they insisted.

Cousin Joseph was now holding evangelistic meetings in different parts of America. This particular trip was to take them across the western United States by car, with another family. They would stay in cheap motels, eat by the side of the road, and trust the Lord to provide through "love offerings" gathered at the end of each meeting.

At first Majken doubted that she had the faith to start out a day with no money and only enough gas to get them to the next meeting. But each evening they were fed, and there was enough money for the motel and the next day's journey. Nightly they knelt together and thanked God for His sufficiency. There was so little in this world that they really needed.

Majken was alert, always watching for those in need. She was impressed by the affluence of the people to whom Joseph ministered. It was evident in their homes, their cars, and even their churches—and often in how little they shared. Majken was certain that none of them ever had outstretched hands or ragged clothes—unless they were clothes they were sending to missionaries.

Returning to Chicago, Majken could not explain how she felt. She only knew that she had taken another significant turn down a path long prepared for her. She returned to her nursing duties with a new sense that something was about to happen.

She learned to love America, amazed at the realm of opportunities she saw all around her and blessed by how cleverly the people utilized their ambitions to better their country. She also learned equality. There was no oligarchy in America. Greatness came not from family lines, but from one's ability to work hard and profit from opportunity.

She made several more trips with Joseph and his family, trips that gave her additional insights into the churches of America. For a fleeting moment during a trip to Mexico she thought she had found her vision in the haunting eyes and the ragged poverty of the children. But not yet . . . maybe someday, but not yet.

More and more she was drawn to stories of European refugees from World War II. There was one problem. She had vowed that Germany was the one place she would never go. She could not forgive the Third Reich for what they had done to her Europe. She held firm. "Lord, anywhere but Germany."

She read about what was happening in Poland and in

Hungary. She saw pictures of Russian troops. She realized that the war was not over for everyone.

With this burden weighing heavily, she felt the need to return to Sweden for a vacation. Within herself she knew that there was much more behind her desire, but a vacation was reason enough for the moment. So, in October, 1953, sure that she belonged in America, but terribly unsure about where God was leading her, she returned to her parents' outstretched arms.

# 4

## IN SEARCH
## OF A VISION

Back in Sweden, Majken spent a few days getting reacquainted with the family. But it wasn't long before she knew she must move on. She felt a sense of urgency about making a trip to the Continent. She had thought she would be content to be back in the familiar surroundings of her beloved homeland, but instead she felt like a pilgrim, just passing through.

Her attention was especially drawn to a home for refugee children that she had been reading about located in Eckernförde, Germany, on the Baltic Sea. She decided to visit the home first, as it was near the Swedish border, and then to spend some time in the refugee camps on the Communist border. She wrote a letter to the director of the home, Rev. Christian Schreiber, an evangelical Lutheran pastor, briefly requesting permission to visit. Then she contacted a travel agency to make arrangements for transportation and accommodations. She had already decided that when she visited these organizations she would take care of her own food and lodgings. After living with her cousins in Chicago, she had discovered that not everyone did. In fact, she often wondered if there were not professional religious tourists who traveled to various parts of the world to "see for themselves" how their mission dollars were being spent, all the while living off the missionaries' meager budgets.

With her arrangements finalized, Majken saw no reason to wait for a response from Pastor Schreiber. She caught an early train and arrived at the rail station in Eckernförde late in the evening. It was mid-October, and the winter wind was already clearing the city center of all but the most hardy citizens.

She scanned the street for a taxi as she took her hotel reservation slip from her purse. She had studied German in school, but with her repulsion of Hitler and the Nazis she had deliberately repressed what little of the language she did know.

She crawled in the back seat of an old cab and silently handed the driver her reservation slip. With a grunt the old man squinted at the paper, glanced skeptically at Majken, then shrugged his shoulders as he nursed the taxi down the street. He never picked up speed, and shortly Majken noticed that she had passed the same sign twice. She leaned forward and showed the driver again the piece of paper with the hotel's name. He grunted, turned down a side street, and in a few moments pulled up in front of a rather dingy-looking guesthouse. In the window glowed a yellow neon sign: *Gotstube*—"cheap rent."

She paid the taxi driver, telling him most decidedly in Swedish that she knew he certainly had taken the long way to get there. He simply shrugged his shoulders and took the money. As he drove off, she felt a rush of panic. *Do I dare go in?* she thought. She heard lusty choruses coming from inside the guesthouse, much like the ones she had heard from the bars when she visited some of the missions in Chicago. The words, "I will never leave you, nor forsake you," buoyed her courage. She lifted her chin, picked up her suitcase, and walked through the door.

The room was hot and dim after the brisk night air, and the smoke hung heavy, mixed with the unmistakable odor of unwashed bodies. She was about to make a quick retreat when she noticed what appeared to be a registration desk.

Ignoring several curious stares, she walked over and handed her reservation slip to the clerk behind the desk. Disinterestedly glancing at the paper, he shoved a torn ledger with a broken pencil across the counter.

It was obvious that reservations were not needed. She quickly signed the register, as the clerk handed her a key and jerked his head toward a staircase to her right. "Thank you," she said in German, but he was already back with his beer.

The staircase led to a dimly-lit hallway. She heard high-pitched giggling from one of the rooms. She found her door, inserted the key, stepped inside, and reached for a light switch. A naked light bulb, hanging in the middle of the room, came to life. She let out a deep sigh and set her suitcase on the floor. *Safe at last,* she thought with relief as she sat on the lumpy bed.

Suddenly she realized how emotionally drained she was. It had been a long day, and she needed rest. She kicked off her shoes, then took off her coat and laid it across the foot of the bed. The room was stuffy but cold. Without undressing further, Majken lifted the blanket back and slid into bed on top of the sheets. She lay rigid, her head slightly elevated by a pillow that was a comfort in name only, and folded her hands over the top of the blanket. *Now I know how the dead feel when they are placed on view,* she thought, *except dead people don't have to contend with the smell.*

*Well,* she said to herself, *here you are, Majken. Lying on a lumpy, mildewed mattress, covered with a blanket that smells like it's been used for a bar cloth downstairs. Here I am in Germany.* She remembered how she had insisted, "Any place but Germany. . . ." *The words are true, aren't they Lord? "Judgment belongs to God." It is not for me to judge a whole nation because of one man.* She heard laughter and the strains of an accordion downstairs, and for a moment she remembered hotly that Hitler had started his career in a beer hall. Then her sense of

32

mission returned. *Well, you have to admit this is better than being in a barn with a donkey and the smell of manure,* she thought with a wry smile.

# 5

# WELCOME
# TO GERMANY

Majken opened one eye. *It's true; I am here,* she thought,
and opened the other eye. The noise from the previous
night was gone, but the odor of mildew and beer remained.
She gingerly lifted the clammy blanket aside, slid out of
bed, and peered out the window to the narrow street below.
People were moving about, bundled in heavy coats against
the cold. Looking at her watch, she was surprised she had
slept so long. It was 8:30.

Shivering as a chill went through her, she went to her
suitcase and took out a small leather bag with her toilet
articles. Her job now was to find a water closet. She unlocked her door and peeked out into the hallway. No traffic.
She stepped out, clutching her bag to her chest, and looked
both ways. Finally she spotted a door ajar at the end of the
hall. Carefully she closed her door behind her, locked it,
and tiptoed toward the open door. Her nose told her what
her mind wasn't sure of. As she got closer, she saw a small
"WC" scrawled across the door. She stepped inside and
pressed into place the bolt that locked the door from the
inside. Nausea rose dangerously in her throat as she surveyed the dimly lit, filthy cubicle. With a determined swallow she quickly made her toilet and returned to her room,
ready to face whatever lay ahead.

Majken had reserved her room for three days. Philosophically she told herself that it wasn't as offensive in the daylight as she had imagined last night. Determined to endure, she put on her hat and coat and headed downstairs. The beer garden was quiet. An old man was walking around with a gunny sack, picking up empty beer mugs. Neither he nor the clerk behind the registration desk paid any heed to Majken or even acknowledged her presence. Even if the beer garden had shown evidence of being a cafe by day, Majken had no appetite.

As she stepped outside the hotel, the early winter morning greeted her drearily. Anger surged inside of her as she looked down the street and saw the rail station two blocks away. That taxi driver had really taken her for a ride last night. *Well, never mind,* she said to herself. She made her way towards the station and a telephone. As she walked, she fumbled in her purse and got out the little address book where she had copiously recorded her itinerary and the names and phone numbers of contacts.

In the train station, she exchanged some money and asked for coins for the telephone, holding her hand by her ear to indicate "telephoning." The clerk handed her some change and pointed to a phone across the waiting room. Deliberately she dialed Herr Schreiber's number and stopped her ear against the echoes of the rail station.

The ringing stopped, and a thick-voiced woman came on the line. *"Ja?"* She was cut off by a rapid beeping, and Majken scrambled to insert a few coins in the machine. Again, *"Ja?"* and then a long pause. Majken searched her mind frantically for the proper German. "Herr Schreiber?"

The reply was a barrage of German, spoken far too fast for Majken to comprehend. Silence, then again, *"Ja?"*

"Herr Schreiber?" asked Majken.

*"Nein, nein,"* came the reply.

"Majken Broby," she said slowly. "Majken Broby."

There was a brief pause at the other end, and then a signal of recognition and another onslaught of German.

"I speak English," said Majken haltingly, carefully enunciating each word. Then she listened intently to the response spoken in broken English.

"*Ja, ja,* Herr Schreiber, he come get Majken Broby, in maybe one hour. *Ja,* he has taken load, load of, how you say, garbage, *ja,* garbage to dump. He pick up Majken Broby on way home."

"I am at the train depot," answered Majken, straining to emphasize each word.

"*Ja, ja.* You stay. He pick up, one hour, train depot."

"I wait," said Majken. "*Auf wiedersehen . . . danke schön!*"

"*Ja, ja,*" came the voice in sing-song at the other end. "*Gut by.*"

Majken placed the phone receiver back in the cradle and turned to walk outside. *Taking a load of garbage to the dump, and he'll pick you up on the way back.* It was raining now, a gray, steady drizzle, the kind that could turn to snow at any time. She moved back under the eaves of the station and waited for Herr Schreiber.

*Well, at least I am expected,* she thought, and then she began to laugh. The thought struck her that Herr Schreiber must be a very practical man. Gasoline was expensive in postwar Germany, and there was no need to make a special trip. Then she wondered, *Was the trip made to pick me up and also dump the garbage, or the other way around?*

She had plenty of time to think about it. One hour, then two. Finally two and a half hours later, when she was beginning to feel that she had been forgotten altogether, she heard her name.

"Fraülein Broby?"

Startled, she looked up. Standing in front of her was a stocky man, a little older than Majken, garbed in baggy trousers, a worn sweater, and a cap. His blue eyes betrayed

36

a reservoir of goodwill, lying just behind the business-like facade.

"Herr Schreiber," she said.

He nodded, then turned and started toward the street. She followed him, saying nothing. They arrived at a gray Volkswagen. Herr Schreiber unlocked the passenger's side and left it open. She got in the car, wondering where he had carried the garbage.

In a few moments they found themselves on a dirt road. The rain had stopped. Herr Schreiber glanced at her several times, and Majken was sure that he was trying to form the right words to speak.

Finally he said, in English, "You speak German?" The *g* was soft, so that he pronounced it "Cherman."

"A tiny bit," said Majken. Then she realized it was more than he understood, so she rephrased it, "Little." The conversation ended.

The Volkswagen began to rattle as he picked up speed, dodging the worst holes in the road and shuddering over the ruts. After another short interval he asked, "You speak Finnish?"

"*Nyet*," said Majken, "only English and Swedish."

Herr Schreiber responded in Swedish. Majken realized as he talked that he had assumed she was an American. She had used American stationery in writing to him and had said she was from Chicago.

Majken was giving him a quick sketch of her life in Swedish when they pulled up to what appeared to be a garbage dump. He backed up the car and abruptly got out. Majken rolled down the window and looked back. Herr Schreiber was attaching a small trailer to the VW. *So,* she realized, *he left the garbage trailer behind while he came to pick me up.* Instantly she gained respect for the man's sensitivity.

Herr Schreiber returned to the wheel, and they drove off. He started to speak but was interrupted by a coughing spell.

37

He held his handkerchief over his mouth until he stopped, then meticulously folded it and put it back in his pocket.

"We are very short of gas. It is very expensive. So I hauled the garbage into town and picked you up at the same time."

As they continued their drive to the children's home, Herr Schreiber confirmed her worst suspicions. "We have many people come here from America," he said. "They come with their expensive clothes and expect us to treat them as important people. They visit our home, they eat our food, they sleep in our beds, and then they say 'Good-bye,' leaving behind only empty promises, or maybe a small gift to 'buy a Bible for the children.' We never hear from them again."

He paused for a moment and looked at Majken expectantly.

Quickly she explained that she had a room in town and would pay for her meals. She told of her interest in his work and the desire to see more of it. She made no promises, other than to assure him she would not be a burden.

From that point, what had begun with all the ingredients of a minor disaster turned into a cordial welcome. Majken realized that Pastor Schreiber was lapsing more and more into German, and so was she. Her repulsion of the language left her as she warmed to this gentle man.

Conversation came easily as they began to speak of children, but Majken noticed that Herr Schreiber continued to cough almost incessantly, holding his handkerchief to his mouth. He was perspiring, and his face was flushed. "You should be home in bed," she said as he stuck the handkerchief back in his pocket again.

"Maybe later," he began, and then stopped as another fit of coughing seized him.

They took a turn off the main road, and within moments the atmosphere became fresher, more free. Though the outskirts of the city were clean, the countryside still showed the scars of war. Instead of being plowed for the winter, entire fields were still unkempt and grown over. Great patches of forest were broken and bent, as if a huge ax had hacked away at the edges. When they turned into the home, Majken noticed by contrast how manicured the landscape was. Every tree seemed to belong, straight and young and new. Each stone set along the roadside seemed to have grown there. A small group of children were running relays on a nearby green. The barrack-type buildings on the property needed paint, but otherwise the setting was meticulous.

The car stopped before a long, low, red-brick building with plain tar paper on the roof. Neat, white window frames gave it the appearance of being well-used but hospitable.

"Majken, I am Sister Ruth. Welcome."

A young woman dressed in the dark blue habit of a Lutheran order extended her hand as Majken got out of the car. She had one of the friendliest smiles that Majken had seen for a long time, exuding such warmth that the last vestiges of her fear and apprehension were chased away. Someone had prepared her visit long in advance.

Sister Ruth led Majken through narrow white double doors to a small entryway, where several children were hanging up their hats and jackets. She noticed how neatly each child placed his notebook underneath his peg.

"We are about to have lunch, and we would like you to join us," said Sister Ruth, as she took Majken's coat. Majken watched with reluctance as her purse was taken and hung over her coat, but a quick look from Sister Ruth assured her it would be safe.

The two women entered a large, spotless room furnished only with dining tables. Six plain chairs were positioned at each table; the white tablecloths were mended but clean. On one wall was a small clock. In the corner, Majken noticed a hanging cross, cut out in the shape of a sword. There were several other wood carvings; one depicting people being tossed about on a stormy sea.

Noticing Majken's interest in the carvings, Sister Ruth said, "A refugee who once visited the home made those for us."

As Majken was directed to a table in the corner, she noticed the children quietly walking in. There was laughter, but Majken remarked that none of them were unruly. As she had expected, several were quite solemn.

Some of the children craned to see the newcomer as several other young people began serving the soup. The first bowl went to Majken, the next to Sister Ruth.

"Pastor Schreiber is not feeling well, so he will not join us today," explained Sister Ruth as she watched the soup bowls being passed around to all the children. When everyone was served, Sister Ruth stood. The room was instantly quiet. She led the children in a short prayer of thanksgiving for the food.

This done, everyone began to eat. Majken noticed that there was no bread and no drink. She sipped the soup, and mentioned to Ruth how good it was.

"You will meet Sister Brünhilda this afternoon. She is a refugee herself. She is getting rather old. It is difficult to know which the children love most, the Sister or her cooking. She always manages to turn one loaf of bread into enough to feed everyone. She makes everything taste good."

A mild hubbub rose in the room as the children chattered at the different tables. Majken was impressed as to how mannerly they were. She was certain that in her own country this many children would have required an adult to supervise every table.

When there was a lull in the conversation, Majken asked Sister Ruth about the home.

"We have refugee children here who come from the bunkers and the cellars."

"Bunkers and cellars?" asked Majken.

"Yes, you will see when you visit them. Atrocious places—no air, no food, and certainly little love."

Sister Ruth continued. "We bring them here and nurse them back to health so that they can go back and be strong enough to at least want to continue to live. We do not have them attend school, as it is such a short stay."

"What do they do all day?" asked Majken, as she fished out the one piece of meat that was floating near the top of her bowl.

"Well," said Sister Ruth, with new enthusiasm in her voice—she never tired of telling about her children. "We awaken everyone at seven. We Sisters go about the house singing gospel songs for them. Some have had long nights with many bad dreams. We want them to be awakened with joy, something better than what they have already experienced. Everyone has a wash and then at 7:30 we meet in this room for breakfast and prayers. Then the children are excused to go into the woods and hunt leaves for Sister Brünhilda's kitchen, or they may go to the sea and pick sea shells."

*Leaves for the kitchen?* thought Majken. *Surely food is not so scarce.* She finished her last spoonful of soup. She was still hungry. She wondered how the children could be full if they had been out playing all morning in the fresh air. As though anticipating the question, Sister Ruth surveyed the children and smiled. "You see, Majken, these children have just had in this one meal as much food as they would receive in two or three days in the bunkers. Their little stomachs have shrunk. True, this might not have been a feast, but to them it was much more than they could have ever dreamed of in the bunkers and cellars."

Sister Ruth stood. All talking immediately ceased and the children joined hands. Bowing their heads they said together, *"Wir danken dem Herrn*—we thank You, Lord, for this food."

41

It was the cue to be excused. The children picked up their bowls, carried them to a table at the end of the room, and left as quietly and orderly as they had entered.

"They are not as strong as they look," said Sister Ruth as she and Majken followed suit. "You see, some have only been here a week. Their bodies still need much rest. So now everyone will go to their beds and rest for two hours."

Sister Ruth led Majken down the hall to a room much the size of the one where they had eaten. There were several large windows hung with colorful curtains down one wall. White painted steel beds were arranged side by side in two neat rows. A couple of the boys were talking in a corner while the rest were crawling into bed. The floor was concrete, painted red. It gave the room a feeling of being lived in. The talk among the boys was gaining when Sister Ruth reminded them, with the big smile with which she had greeted Majken, that it was time to rest. There was some resistance from the corner, but that ended with a look from Sister Ruth.

Sister Ruth led Majken to another room at the other end of the hallway. It was the same size, with the same kind of beds in two long rows, but the curtains were prettier. The girls were already quiet.

"Would you like to rest, or would you like a quick tour of our home?" asked Sister Ruth.

"Oh, I am far too excited to rest. Could I see more?" Sister looked pleased as she handed Majken her coat and purse and they went out the front door. They walked briskly down the stone drive, then stopped at the gate to survey the home. Its two buildings were set on a high hill, which rose just a little above the Baltic Sea. Beyond the barracks lay a forest of tall fir.

"You see, our children can either play in the woods on one side, or go down to the sea."

They began to walk towards the sea, and Sister Ruth

continued her narrative, "Pastor Schreiber and his family are refugees themselves. The British army occupied these barracks, but when they left the German government gave them to Herr Schreiber to house orphans. Much work had to be done. The buildings were rundown, and they didn't look much like homes. We were afraid that the children would not think of them as much better than the bunkers and the cellars.

"Pastor Schreiber and some other refugees went to work and cut out large windows, laid stone walkways, felled trees, and now you see what we have. Everything here was built by the hands of refugees."

Majken had many questions, and before they were aware of it, it was time for the children to get up. Sister Ruth suggested that Majken borrow Pastor Schreiber's diary to learn more of the "early days."

As they returned to the main house, they could hear the shouts of children. Sister Ruth hurried her pace. "We now have the afternoon Bible story hour. This is the part of the day that the children look forward to the most. Pastor Schreiber usually tells the stories, but today I'll substitute."

Sister Ruth was right. The children listened to the Bible stories with rapt attention. After it was over they were given an opportunity to ask questions, and then there was a time of singing. For almost thirty minutes they sang gospel songs, as the children clamored for verse after verse.

"Why do you enjoy singing so much?" Majken asked a little girl beside her. The child looked to be about eight, with ragged but clean blonde hair. She had been especially enthusiastic during the singing.

The child looked at Majken as though it was a question that should never have had to be answered. "Why? Because it makes my heart happy."

Majken understood. The entire place seemed to make people's hearts happy. The loving atmosphere never faltered as they played together, talked in little groups, and then returned for the evening meal at six o'clock. The supper was simple, but the children seemed satisfied: one piece of black bread with lard and a cup of hot cocoa.

Again the prayers, the thanksgiving, and then cleanup before bedtime. By seven the children were all in bed, and the Sisters went from child to child, praying with each one individually.

Tired but happy, Majken returned to her hotel room. The smell was suffocating after the freshness of the country, and another raucous celebration was going on in the beer garden downstairs. But Majken had more important things to do than to complain. What she had seen at the home had so filled her heart, mind, and soul that she had to know more.

She crawled into bed, fully clothed, propped a pillow behind her, pulled the blanket over her legs and opened Pastor Schreiber's diary. It had been a parting gift from Sister Ruth—"Until tomorrow," she had promised.

Oblivious to the cold and the dim lighting, Majken began to read.

Today Sister Ruth came to me with the little box in which we keep our money. She asked me to open it. There was one mark and fifty pfennigs.* Anxiety gripped my heart. This was reality. All these children to feed on one mark. I put the box on the table and beside it I put the Bible. Faith in God's Word and reality— one mark—lay side by side.

In the kitchen we had four pounds of sugar, two loaves of bread, and half a sack of grain. Fifteen children had to be fed, three of them my own children. We made up a menu. In the morning each one had two dry, very thin slices of bread with one teaspoon of sugar. For dinner Sister Brünhilda made soup from the tops of sugar beets and some grain. In the evening, she cooked more soup from the grain. When we ate the last of the soup and gathered the crumbs of the bread with our fingers, the

---

*About twenty-five cents.

prayer was still ringing in our ears: "Our Father, give us today our daily bread."

Everyone kept busy to prepare for more starving children from the camps. From sacks that had been used by the military for flour, we made sheets and pillowcases. We made mattresses and put straw inside. Also pillows in the same way. Sister Ruth said they were not soft enough, so she worked diligently on them, reminding us that they were for precious little heads.

During this time of hardship, my faith was severely tested. The Lord had helped us to get building material. What had happened now? Had God left us? Then one day as I read in my Bible, I felt like the Lord spoke directly to me. It was Hebrews, chapter 12, verses 5 and 6.

"My son, do not think lightly or scorn to submit to the correction and discipline of the Lord, nor lose courage and give up and faint, when you are reproved or corrected by Him. For the Lord corrects and disciplines every one whom He loves and He punishes, even scourges, every son whom He accepts and welcomes to His heart and cherishes."*

Majken could understand that verse; she had read it often enough herself. She gathered the blanket to her chest.

I had hardly finished reading these words before I understood that this was God's answer to me. I had wavered between faith and doubt. In these words the Lord showed me that He loved us! He had not left us!

I went and got the box. There was the mark and the pfennigs. In the kitchen we had only two slices of bread. But I felt happy. Faith in God had returned to me.

Majken paused to consider the importance of what she had read. Then, she turned the page and continued.

Next day was Sunday. Someone knocked on my door. A man dressed in uniform was standing outside. He gave me a telegram. There was no money, but the words in the telegram were

---

*AMPLIFIED.

gold to us. An old friend of mine, a missionary from Africa, had sent this message from Hannover asking, "Can you accept sixty children? We bring food with us." The prayer for both children and food had been answered.

It was good that the reply was prepaid, for I had no money. I ran to the post office in Eckernförde and telegraphed: "All of you are welcome!"

We did not have sixty beds for sixty children, but we had to arrange something. Two days later, English military trucks stopped outside the children's home. Children and food were unloaded.

In the kitchen, as I write this, the big pots are filled. The wonderful smell of boiling potatoes pervades the house. We will eat as much as we dare, and then in the morning we will eat the rest for breakfast.

Majken closed the diary for a moment. *Could I exercise this kind of faith?* She asked herself. *Could I spend everything I have and throw myself upon just a few words, like "Give us this day our daily bread?"*

She was afraid to search out the answer. Instead she turned back to the diary.

We have no food for the children. We have used up the last of our grain. We believe God will supply in time for the noon meal . . . Shortly after I wrote this a truck pulled up. A driver got out and said that he had some wheat that he was taking to the dump. Would we like it for our pigs? We had a couple of pigs that we were raising in a sty out back. I told him yes. He warned us that the grain was rotten and might poison people if they ate it, but it was safe for the pigs. He threw two sacks off the truck and a couple of children moved them to the pig sty. It was then that they discovered the driver had made a mistake. He had left us two sacks of perfectly good wheat that were to be delivered to a bakery for flour. The children told me, and I caught the driver just as he was going out the gate. I told him of his mistake, but he shouted back, "That's okay. You keep it. I will stand good for it." In a few hours we had a delicious dinner.

Majken's heart felt as if it would explode. Her eyes burned and her back was stiff with cold. She did not know

46

how long she had been reading. The beer garden was quiet. She laid the diary down, her mind jumbled with questions. The answers were lost in sleep.

For the next two days, Majken continued to read the diary and visit the home. Her relationship with Sister Ruth solidified as she played with the children and listened quietly to the talk about the home. As Majken was leaving the third evening, she asked the question that had persisted since her arrival. "Sister Ruth, I have noticed that you have a room with forty beds in it, but it is empty. Why is that?"

Sister Ruth's head dropped, and a sadness encompassed her usually positive countenance. "Because, Sister Majken, we have no money to feed forty more children. I would take in hundreds if I could."

The idea that there were empty beds at the home while the cellars and bunkers were still full of children tore at Majken's heart. There were children who were starving and cold, much like those she had come to love in the past three days—children who needed what such a home could offer. *This cannot be!* she thought. *The world is so much better—the economy is burgeoning. The war has been over for nearly a decade. Surely there can't be more children like this. Maybe Sister Ruth and Herr Schreiber are wrong. Maybe the cellars and the bunkers no longer exist. They couldn't in a Christian world . . . people would not allow it to happen.*

Majken had to know for herself. She went back to her room and packed her bags. Under Herr Schreiber's arrangements she would see these refugee camps.

47

# 6

## "COME HELP US"

The war had been over for eight years. Since the cessation of hostilities, a new war had begun in Europe. Its victims were the eighteen million East Europeans who voted for freedom with their feet and were fleeing from the countries given to the Soviet Union as bounty for the hunt called World War II.

Millions could not escape and were driven from their ancestral homes in Latvia, Estonia, and the Ukraine. Trainloads of Poles, Hungarians, Czechs, and East Germans were shipped deep into the interior of the Soviet Union. Fourteen million were buried in some unmarked grave in a forest or put aboard cattle trains and shipped away to a living hell in a Soviet labor camp. There they became numbered parts of the new "glorious" industrial machine, the largest and most treacherous prison ever conceived in the mind of man.

Majken's tour was to include the entire eastern border area of Germany, a wide strip of land reaching from the Baltic Sea to the Austrian Alps. Her guide was a German worker whom Herr Schreiber had arranged to meet her at the airport at Hamburg.

Their first stop was Braunschweig, a city of three hundred thousand, located thirty miles from what was coming

48

to be known as the "Iron Curtain." Braunschweig had been nearly destroyed during the war. Land mines were still being exploded by farmers in the fields or by laborers in the reconstruction of burned-out buildings. But the city was attempting to return to normalcy.

The social worker, Frau Trebing, avoided Majken's attempts at personal conversation. Instead, in tones which hovered between boredom and disdain she relentlessly dictated a list of statistics that first astonished, then overwhelmed Majken by their magnitude.

"There are twenty-six thousand refugees here, in a total of sixty-six camps."

"Twenty-six thousand?" asked Majken, hoping that she had heard wrong.

"Those are only the ones we know about," continued Frau Trebing. "Those who finally make it across the border represent only a fraction of those who try to escape from the Soviet sector. You will also find that not all refugees register. Many simply stay on as illegal immigrants. They actually number in the millions."

She glanced obliquely at Majken.

"We can turn around and go back if you like."

"No," said Majken, startled out of her reflections. "I must see all that I can . . . I must see them."

"Very well, we shall see 'them,' " replied Frau Trebing with a trace of irony in her voice. She brought the car to a stop in front of what Majken guessed was a former gun placement. It stood about four stories high and was windowless. There was one small door cut out of the cement. It was cold, and there were only a few people outside—bedraggled, half-dressed men, women, and children listlessly shuffling around in front of the building. *Surely,* thought Majken, *those inside must be better off.* No one seemed to pay any attention to the two women as they got out of the car. Majken wondered if this was an everyday event. Had they been given hope so many times that they could not stand one more disappointment?

"This was once a bunker," explained Frau Trebing as they picked their way across the frozen mud.

"A bunker . . . ?" asked Majken.

"An air raid shelter, or at least it used to be," replied the social worker in the same noncommittal voice. "Now it's a home for refugees. The walls are four yards deep. The space inside has about the same measurements."

A couple of young children huddled together on the ground moved aside as Majken and Frau Trebing started through the entrance. Majken stopped abruptly as the stench inside hit her like a chloroform pad. Frau Trebing looked at her with the first obvious sign of concern.

Majken pressed her hand over her nose and backed away. A young man leaving the shelter pushed her gently aside. Then she took a deep breath and nodded to Frau Trebing.

It took a few moments for Majken's eyes to adjust inside the shelter. A few grimy light bulbs gave the only light. The glaring contrast in the darkness made her eyes ache. Along the left-hand wall stood a long line of women with their backs turned to them. Electrical cords dangled above them to the ceiling.

"Those are hot plates for the families to cook their food. Each plate is used by six or eight families," Frau Trebing explained as they made their way across the room. "As you can see, they are in constant use."

To the right were strung rows and rows of clothes and blankets, haphazard partitions to mark off the living quarters.

"May I speak to some of them?" asked Majken.

"Oh yes, though not many will want to talk. They have been through much, and they are not terribly trusting."

For the first time Majken noticed a tinge of sorrow in the

social worker's voice. *Maybe,* thought Majken, *she's only protecting herself. She will bring someone else here tomorrow, and the next day, and the next. Maybe this is how she remains rational.* She turned and surveyed the incredible scene before her.

*And these people are called free,* she thought. *Free from what, free for what? What must it be like on the other side, if they leave it all for this?*

Majken pulled back one partition, a torn piece of gray blanket, gritty to the touch. Sitting on a bed was a woman staring fixedly into space. Majken could only guess how old she was—maybe thirty, maybe forty. She bent down and touched her shoulder. No response.

"How are you?" inquired Majken sympathetically. Slowly the woman turned her head. Her eyes were hollow. The scarf on her head slipped to her shoulders as she moved. Her hair was as ragged as her clothes. *Her body looks thirty, but her eyes look ninety,* thought Majken.

"How long have you been here?" she asked, trying to coax some response.

The woman held up five fingers.

"Five . . .?" asked Majken.

She nodded mechanically.

"Five days or five weeks?" asked Majken.

For the first time her eyes focused, and she looked deeply into Majken's own.

"No, lady, five years." She held up the five fingers again, then dropped her hand and sank back into her own world. Involuntarily Majken stretched her hand toward the woman, but the social worker took her elbow. "That's all you will find out. Come, let's move on."

Majken walked away reluctantly, glancing back at the woman. *Five years . . . Lord, why? What hope does she have?*

She stumbled over something sticking out from under a curtain. She looked down and saw that she had tripped over a small, bony foot. Majken knelt down and gingerly lifted the blanket. There was a little girl, maybe five or six years old. Majken had been a nurse long enough to know the signs of advanced tuberculosis. The child began to cough as Majken quickly dropped the rag and hurried to follow the social worker.

They took a small stairway up to the second floor. With each step the stench became more unbearable.

"Let's take a look in here," said Frau Trebing, opening a small door. She motioned for Majken to go inside.

The room was small, maybe five yards square. Three narrow beds were pushed together and covered with urine-soaked mattresses. There was no other furniture. Sitting on the beds were a woman and six children.

At their entrance the mother, hair disarrayed, showed signs of what was once a beautiful smile. She stood, looked at Majken and then at the children and spoke.

"You have come to help us." Was it a request, or a report that it was too late?

"I hope that I can help you," said Majken as she moved towards the children. "I hope that I can help," she murmured again as she reached down to stroke one of the drooping heads. The social worker stood at the door, betraying no sign of emotion.

The mother moved closer, and the odor of sweat and urine caused nausea to sweep momentarily over Majken. *I must not give false hope,* she thought. *I must not destroy whatever thread of hope they have left. Please, Lord, tell me what to say.*

The mother began to speak.

"Five months ago we fled from the other side. This is all we brought," and she pointed to the children. "They have been kind enough to give us these," she half smiled as she pointed to the beds. "We are so thankful that we do not have to sleep on the cement floors like so many others. It is very cold, and the children get pneumonia. . . ."

*Thankful,* thought Majken. *Thankful . . .*

"You will have to excuse my children. They do not look so good," she said apologetically. "But my husband is very sick and in the hospital, and I am all alone."

"But . . ." Majken wanted to ask how she lived, but the woman continued, almost as in a trance.

"They are very kind to us. They give us thirty-two marks* a week. We pay for our room and for our heat and light, and the rest we use to buy some potatoes. Sometimes there is even enough for bread. But never meat.

"Someday," she continued, almost to herself, "I must buy bad potatoes and mildewed bread, to have a few pfennigs left over to buy milk."

She pointed to a tiny baby asleep on one of the beds.

Majken gazed from mother to child.

"He is ten," said the mother pointing to another child. "And that is his twin brother beside him. Friedrich is not very healthy. We worry about him."

Compassion welled up in Majken's heart as the children gathered tightly around their mother.

"She is eight, she is five, he is three, and our little son, who is sleeping, is eight months old. But he sleeps too much. We are beginning to worry about him, also."

She stepped over to the bed where the baby was asleep and knelt down beside him. "He sleeps too much. We are worried," she repeated, caressing the downy head.

Majken escaped to the door. In the hall she pressed against the cold cement wall, trying to regain her composure. Her hands dropped limply to her sides as she muttered, "Lord, Lord . . ." Nothing more would come out.

Majken was jerked back to reality as a woman jostled her rudely. She was clutching her throat, rasping in a whisper to anyone who would listen. "My goiter . . . I cannot get air in my room. I must get air." She pushed her way down the

---

*About eight dollars.

small corridor, followed by curses as she bumped others along the way.

The social worker, now a bit more sympathetic, led Majken up another flight of stairs. The air was even more stifling. They stopped in front of another small room and looked inside. A gaunt, ragged man, not more than thirty years old, stood in the middle of the floor, crooning brokenly in Polish to the babe in his arms. The child was wrapped in a piece of carpet. He turned to stare at the intruders. Three children clung to his legs. They showed no signs of fear, only baleful curiosity.

There were two small beds in the room, one stacked on top of the other. As Majken moved closer, she noticed a woman huddled in the corner. She was sitting on the cold concrete floor, mending some tattered clothes.

Majken moved toward her, and she looked up. Though her face was no more than a girl's, her eyes were ancient, empty, burned out. Pitifully she raised her bony hands, and compassionately Majken grasped them to her breast. The woman's face was as gray as the bunker walls; her hands as cold as the cement floor.

She stared into Majken's eyes for a moment and then looked down and returned to her mending. It was then that Majken saw that she had neither needle nor thread in her hands. She backed up to the door. The husband's face registered immeasurable pain as he looked first at his wife, then at Majken—pain of failure as a father, as a husband, as a human being. Majken quickly left the room.

One more flight of stairs. Again the sickening stench, but by now all that registered was a searing pain in Majken's soul.

The top floor was one big room. It housed more than fifty young people who had been taken off the street. They were not drunkards or beggers, but adolescents bereft of father and mother. They were potential doctors, lawyers, musicians, painters. But now they were locked away as part of a vast human cargo, drifting into oblivion as refugees. Majken thought of the empty beds back at the home in Eckernförde.

Her attention was drawn to a beautiful teen-ager whose milky complexion framed deep blue eyes. Her blonde hair, though unkempt, showed signs of being combed by her fingers. With difficulty Majken crossed the room to where the girl sat on the floor. She looked up at her.

"Where are you from?" asked Majken.

"Estonia," came the quiet reply.

"Do you have a mother or a father?" asked Majken.

"No, they are dead . . . both are dead. I am the only one left." The girl bowed her head. Majken knelt beside her and strained to hear as each word came, pushed by pain. "When I was ten—I am now nineteen—my foster mother was killed in a bomb raid, and four of us children were left alone.

"The following day the Communists came and took us as prisoners. We were thrown into a room with many other people. Then the soldiers came." She paused for a minute, searched Majken's face, then bent her head down again as she continued her story. "The Communist soldiers came and took many young girls for themselves. One," she looked again at Majken, "one was my sister."

Majken caressed her cheek, and the girl looked at her.

"She never came back." Her voice became more intense, shaded with a bitterness paradoxical with the angelic face. "We saw it all from the window. We knew we would never see them again. The soldiers were merciful. . . ." Again she looked Majken straight in the eye. "The soldiers were merciful. They shot the girls at the end of the day."

Majken's hand dropped limply to her knee. The girl reached over and held it tenderly, staring at the hand as she talked. "My other sister and I escaped with our brother. But somehow we became separated; I have never seen them since that day. The Communists captured me, and I was sent to work in the mines." Her voice became husky as she continued. "For days at a time, I stood in water up to here." She held her hand up to her knees. "It was a mineral mine. Many died." She paused and released Majken's hand, then hugged her knees to her chest. "So you see, this is not bad here." She nodded towards the rest of the room. "At least there are no soldiers. Later I escaped and was captured. Again, I was sent to a slave labor camp. . . ." A grim smile crossed her face. "But again I escaped. There were so many of us they could not watch us all. I escaped across the border, and now, I am free. I am no longer afraid." She rested her chin on her knees. "But I miss my brothers and sisters." She shrugged after a silence. "I guess I will get along without them too."

Majken knelt and embraced her, but the girl did not respond.

Another makeshift cubicle; another woman in rags surrounded by children.

"Why did you leave your home to come to this?" asked Majken.

"I love my children," said the mother, as though all the world would understand. "I could not permit what they were teaching my children.

"Each day my children had to recite the Lord's Prayer with Stalin's name inserted instead of God's. They also were told to pray to God for food, candy, or a toy. When they opened their eyes, there would be nothing there, and the teacher would say, 'See, there is no God.' The next day they would be told to pray to Father Stalin for the same thing. When they opened their eyes, there would be the answer to their prayer. 'You see,' the teacher would say, 'Father Stalin hears you, but that other God does not.'

"I had no choice. I could not let the Communists steal the souls of my children. I am *glad* to be here."

*Glad to be here,* thought Majken. Her mind went back to her comfortable little apartment in Chicago . . . the freedom she had to be herself. How little it cost her to be a Christian.

The social worker pulled her gently aside. "Better wait a minute or you will be run over."

A mass of people—young, old, men, women—swept by. Majken and Frau Trebing pressed themselves against a damp cement wall until the rush passed. It was over as suddenly as it had begun.

"What is it?" asked Majken, as she moved away from the wall.

"Air," replied Frau Trebing. "Once each day for a few minutes they pump fresh air into the building, and the people run to the ventilators to have first chance at it."

*Air,* thought Majken. *The world is full of air, and yet here are these people fighting for the air they need to breathe.*

As Majken and Frau Trebing descended the stairs, they could see people pushing, shoving, cursing, still trying to get next to the ventilator. Outside, a chorus of moans went up from the building. The pumps had been shut down for another day.

Neither Majken nor the social worker spoke as they got back into the car and headed for another refugee center. This time it was a city of cardboard huts. They got out of the car and went over to one of the dwellings. It was so small they could only stick their heads inside.

Majken saw an old man get up off the "floor"—the ground covered with newspapers. "I just patched the roof. I am seventy-four, but I am not worthless." He pointed with a shaking hand to a new piece of cardboard pressed over a hole.

"We are but sojourners, strangers in a foreign land," he said humbly as a couple of children looked up from the bed listlessly. "Someday, our strife will be over."

"Yes, someday," said the social worker. "Someday. . . ."

She turned away, but Majken heard her as she muttered bitterly, "But when? When?"

More huts, more people who had exhausted their last supply of hope. Others were too young to fully realize the hopelessness, their constant companion.

Back to another bunker, no better, no worse than all the others. Barefooted children, the terrible stench, and always the babies.

*A grownup can suffer because he understands,* said Majken to herself, *but the children . . . the poor children.*

On the wall of one of the bunkers was a piece of cloth with the words embroidered, "Lord, abide with us: for it is toward evening."

. . . toward evening. To Uelzen—more TB, anemia; to Wentorf—more of the same, 11,440 refugees with nowhere to go. . . .

A frail elderly woman with no teeth spoke for them all. "My husband disappeared in the war, sixteen years ago. I believe he lives. I have hope. See, look," she said, as she gestured to a little table beside the bed. It was set with crude plates and silverware for two. "Someday he will come and sit right here. I always sleep on only one side of my bed, so that if he should come in the night, he can claim what is his . . . in case he comes in the night."

"May it be soon," Majken whispered to herself.

For six weeks Majken continued her travels: southern Germany, on into Austria and Greece. Everywhere the picture was the same. Constantly she prayed that her conscience would not become hardened to what she was seeing. Each time she looked into the face of a refugee she prayed that she would see it as for the first time.

Finally she found herself exhausted and running a fever, at Templehof Airport in West Berlin. The city personified the postwar tension: Sitting in the middle of Soviet-occupied territory, Berlin itself was divided, half Communist, half free.

Wearily she boarded her flight back to Sweden. But even on the plane there was no respite. Refugee women and children filled most of the seats. The plane was silent; the tension almost unbearable.

Majken found her seat and sat down beside a woman holding a toddler in her lap. A boy of about fourteen sat in the window seat. They could see that Majken was not one of them. The boy stared at her with suspicion. Majken smiled at the mother and fastened her seat belt. "My, what a beautiful child," she said, in an attempt to ease their anxiety.

The lady shifted the younger boy to her shoulder and began to talk.

"We lost everything we had. We managed a clothing store. Then one day a young man who was called into the Communist police force came to us. He was a good friend. We knew his family well. He said that he had been ordered to the border, and that he could not shoot and kill innocent people. He asked us to give him some civilian clothes so that he, too, could escape. My husband could not turn him down. The desire for freedom is all one thinks about. We go to sleep with it on our mind, we dream that we have it, and then wake up to find out that we haven't. My husband gave him the clothes. A few hours later they came and took my husband away. The young man, the friend of our family, was working for the Communists. I have never seen my husband since that day."

The roar of the engines interrupted them, and the plane taxied down the runway. In seconds they were airborne, and the pilot announced that they were on their way to Hamburg.

The plane erupted with applause. Many danced into the aisle, hugging each other and raising their hands in joy. Others sat silently, smiling, but with tears streaming down their faces.

The woman reached over and embraced Majken impulsively. "Now, we are free!" she whispered fervently, her face wet with tears. "It is what my husband would have wanted us to do." She held up her youngest as the older boy looked on lovingly. "Now, my children, we are free!" Mother and sons hugged each other tightly, rocking and crooning in the age-old rhythm of comfort.

Majken fell back into her seat, exhausted. Her head throbbed and her forehead was burning. But her mind could not rest. The faces that she had encountered during the past weeks rose, unbidden, before her. She saw the cardboard huts, the concrete bunkers. She smelled the stench. Her head pounded with increased frenzy. She opened her eyes. The mother and her children were looking out the window. Majken reached into the purse still on her lap and took out her notebook. She began to reread the notes she had scribbled:

"My father came back from prison to Siberia. He found my mother and me. My mother was sick and she died. Now he is dead, and I am alone."

"I have lost my legs—frostbitten. My father and brother were shot. My mother and little sister froze to death. I am now twenty years old. . . ."

"I have always wanted to learn things. We tried to flee to the West, but we were captured. My mother and sister and I were sent to Asia, to hard labor camp. We had to keep quiet about our faith. What my sister and I have heard about God was only what my mother told us. During the years we prayed and hoped to one day reach West Germany. Now we are here. Faith in God gave us purpose and hope."

The words began to run together: *Bunkers, mother shot, the border death zone.* "*We lost my mother as we were running from them. We have never found her,*" *cardboard house* . . . The words tumbled in every corner of Majken's mind.

Was there any hope? She thought about the empty beds at Eckernförde. *But there are so many!* she cried to herself. *Yes,* a quiet voice answered, *there are so many. But that is a beginning.*

She wiped the perspiration from her brow and finally allowed her mind to do what it had screamed to do since that first day. Tears began to run down her face as she released all her thoughts and allowed the vision to take over. The wide streets now carried signs, the names of camps all across Germany; the empty eyes pleading for help now had names; the wringing hands were attached to real people, people she had touched. Now she could also hear what they were saying: "Come help us. . . ."

Her mind focused on one of the bombed-out churches where she had stopped to pray. In the front was a statue of Jesus. It too had been damaged: One arm and one hand were missing. Beneath it someone had scrawled the words: "Are you willing to give Me your hands and your arms?"

Majken was willing.

# 7

# THE POWER
# OF THE CROSS

Majken arrived at her parents' home in Sweden, shivering, perspiring, and coughing from pneumonia. For three weeks her mother nursed her back to health.

It was not time lost. As Majken's temperature subsided and she could breathe without her lungs burning, she began to formulate plans.

There was no doubt in her mind that she was being called to work with Herr Schreiber and the home in Eckernförde. Nor was there any doubt that she had come upon the flesh-and-blood reality of her vision. She thought of how that vision, nine years before, had been indelibly impressed in her mind, like one frame in a film frozen momentarily into still life. As she visited the borders and saw the deplorable conditions, the film had become animated. The actors and actresses were men and women, but mostly children, staring at Majken with eyes filled with despair, fear, and helplessness. It was as if someone had turned on the projector, and there she was in the middle of a theater. But Majken knew the movie would not end. She could go back home, but she could never forget what she had seen.

At times she tossed on her pillow, exhausted, and argued, *But I am only one, Lord, and I am only a woman. I don't know anyone who can help.* And then she remembered how her vision had ended. The words had come to her three times: *The power of the Cross, the power of the Cross, the power of the Cross.*

Slowly but with certainty, Majken began to realize that she was only to be a channel through which the power of the resurrected Christ would work.

She thought of the statue of Jesus, without arms or hands. She brought her own hands out from under the covers to look at them as she repeated the words written beneath the statue: "Will you be My arms and My hands?"

Her heart ached when she thought about the parents in those refugee camps; but when she thought about the children, her eyes filled with tears.

*A child's world,* she told herself, *should be a world of trust and love, filled with happy experiences, uninhibited joy, anticipation, security, and other good things.* But she had seen that a child's world can also mean fear, pain, and loneliness.

*Lord, I have seen so many of those in pain, suffering from fear and loneliness. I commit my life to bringing them into a world of trust and love. But Father, I am alone. What can I do?* asked Majken. The words came back gently: *You can help one child. And you can inspire another to good works to help one more child. That is all I ask.*

Slowly Majken regained enough strength to leave her bed. She was content to sit before the fire in the great room, stitching some handwork or studying her Bible. One morning as she was thus occupied, there was a knock on the door. Her mother came out of the kitchen, wiping her hands on her apron. Majken rose as she heard the familiar voice in the entryway. "Majken, Rev. Larson is here to visit with you."

Pastor Gunar Larson had long been a close friend of the family. He had been a great comfort when her father had died earlier in the year, and he had visited with her several times during the past weeks. He sat down and faced Majken squarely, placing his hands resolutely on his knees. Her soul sensed that this was not just a kindly call on a sick friend.

"Majken, you have seen much during your time on the Continent."

"Yes," Majken agreed. "Yes, I have."

"I think that you should come to my church and share with our people that which you have experienced."

She was taken aback. "I . . . I don't know. I have never stood before people before, and I am a woman."

Pastor Larson would not be sidetracked. "Majken, when can you come?" He turned to her mother, who had taken a chair across from Majken. "She looks well enough now, Sigrid. Is she?"

"I think so," said Mrs. Broby quietly.

Majken looked at her mother, then at Pastor Larson. "I will think about it."

Pastor Larson hadn't walked all the way from the bus stop to go away with "maybe." He stood up, hat in hand, and spoke confidently. "I am happy you can come. I have scheduled you for one week from tonight, at seven o'clock. We will look forward to hearing from you. God bless you." Smiling broadly he took his leave.

The visit had lasted only a few minutes, but Majken was filled with apprehension. "It's happening too fast," she told her mother.

Mrs. Broby came over and put her arm around her daughter's shoulders. "The power of the Cross, Majken . . ." She didn't have to say it three times.

Majken got out her writing pad. She sat pensively before the fire—for how long she did not know—and then summarized a set of rules by which she would abide for the rest of her days:

> Never ask for money. Only let the people know what the Lord is going to do. People must give as the Lord speaks to them, not as they are instructed by me.

64

All the money that comes in must go to the work, not to overhead. There will be no large staff, no big offices.

I am only the arms and hands. I only pass to the children what other people give for them.

Don't go around asking to speak. Trust the Lord to have people come to you. They will ask you to come and tell about the needs and the work. Let this ministry multiply only as it comes from the hand of the Lord, like the fishes and the loaves Jesus broke before the five thousand.

A week later, with these ideals uppermost in her mind, she stood before Pastor Larson's congregation. She told of what she had seen, beginning with the home in Eckernförde, and then she took the people on a journey through the cellars and bomb shelters of Germany.

She left with only a small offering; but more important, she realized she could do it. She could stand in front of people and communicate her experiences in terms that they could understand.

When she arrived home, her mother had coffee waiting before the fire. Together they sipped the strong, fragrant drink and discussed how the people had responded.

"Is it right not to ask for money?" asked Majken finally, a small frown furrowing her eyebrows as she concentrated her thoughts. She had not shared her ideas on the subject with anyone.

The words of her mother solidified her philosophy. "Majken, tell the people what the Lord is going to do," she said, leaning forward serenely. "He will find His hands and arms."

That evening Majken also called Herr Schreiber in Eckernförde. Their conversation was lengthy, as Majken explained her thoughts of the previous weeks and her desire to help the home.

After she hung up the phone she looked at her pad. She had jotted down the major priorities that Herr Schreiber had presented.

First, they must fill the forty-four empty beds.

Second, a new wing was needed on the north end of the main building. That would give them room for twenty more beds.

This would mean that sixty-four children could be taken out of the bunkers and off the streets and be given six weeks of food, medical care, and the special kind of love that only the home could give them.

She had her first projects. She had told Herr Schreiber that she would raise the money but had not dared to ask how much it would cost.

Within days, Majken was amazed at how many people started dropping by the house, people she had not seen in years. "You have been on my mind lately," they said. "I just happened to be in the neighborhood, so I thought I would drop by." Some left small gifts.

Each had heard about the refugees and the home and wanted to know more. The forty-four beds and the new wing on the building were something that could be done right now, she explained.

Early one morning a friend whom she had not seen for some time arrived. She had planned a birthday party for another woman and wanted Majken to take "just a few minutes" at the celebration to tell what she had seen in "those terrible refugee camps."

Majken went. The food was wonderful, the fellowship equally good. But no one offered to help. She left feeling that she had said the wrong thing. *Maybe I talked too long. Maybe I should have kept quiet.* Negative thoughts flooded her mind. She had been to other meetings and had talked to numerous people, but she had only a few krona to mail to Herr Schreiber. "Hardly postage money," she told herself, imagining how disappointed he would be when he opened the letter.

Her mood, which hovered between apprehension and wounded pride, was interrupted by another visitor. An aunt, who had been present at the birthday party, arrived unexpectedly. They visited politely for several hours, but no mention was made of the birthday party, the refugees, or even Majken's travels. At last, as she was readying to leave, she quietly slid an envelope from her purse. Majken sensed that her aunt was doing something that she had never done before. Embarrassed, her aunt pressed the paper into Majken's hand and left the room quickly. Tears came to Majken's eyes as she counted out one thousand krona.* This was a large amount of money, and her aunt was not rich. "That is enough to fill the empty beds immediately!" she exclaimed joyfully and headed for the telephone. Herr Schreiber was equally ecstatic, and together they discussed the new wing.

"How much will it cost?" she asked.

"Three thousand dollars!" he replied.

She was incredulous. "That is more than ten times what I am sending you today." She was silent for a moment. "Herr Schreiber, start buying the materials. God will supply."

More gifts came into Majken's hands. All were unexpected, all unsolicited. She immediately posted them to Eckernförde.

Herr Schreiber wrote back. "The children are very excited. They want to know where every brick is coming from. Together we are seeing God perform a miracle before our very eyes. This is a great lesson for the children, as well as for us all."

But the doorbell stopped ringing. There was no mail. Doubts began to creep into Majken's mind. She would wake in the middle of the night, asking herself, *What have I done?* Not only had she agreed to help supply daily bread for forty-four refugees, but she had said she would raise three thousand dollars. The battle with fear sometimes continued through the night.

---

*Two hundred fifty dollars.

One morning she was so defeated she could hardly get out of bed. Sigrid, possessing a great gift of mercy, noticed how worn her daughter looked. She knew what was wrong.

"Majken, let us pray together," she suggested gently.

Together they knelt in the middle of the great room floor. Quietly, Mrs. Broby opened their petitions. "Father, what we bring to You, You already know. Majken is discouraged, and she needs encouragement. She needs Your supply, Your guidance. Please give it to her. . . ."

When she had finished, Majken started to pray, but was interrupted by the telephone's ringing. With a gesture of impatience Majken went to the phone. It was the voice of a very old woman.

"Where can I find Majken Broby? Is she in Germany now, or America, or where?"

"I am here," answered Majken. "This is Majken Broby."

A few moments of silence at the other end of the line, and then a quavering voice said, "You do not know me, but I heard you speak one night. I would like to talk to you. Can we visit?"

Majken made an appointment to meet her the next morning at the bus station in a small village nearby.

The woman was waiting when Majken drove up to the station. She was quite old and poorly dressed, with a wrinkled face, and it was with some effort that she walked over to Majken.

"You are Majken Broby?"

Majken acknowledged the greeting as the woman took her hand and squeezed it warmly. The woman's fingers were cool and bony, her palm hard with callouses. "Come," said the woman. "I live not far from here. We will have some coffee and talk."

As they drove to her home, they talked about the weather. Majken sensed that she needed company; she simply called herself "Old Svea" and said that she had few friends or relatives.

*Well,* thought Majken, *there are all kinds of refugees, including those who are discarded by society. The callouses get too big, and the back is too bent to be of any more use.*

The ache in Majken's heart was matched by the anger that boiled up as she saw where the woman lived. It was little more than a shack, ugly, squat, set alongside a row of shacks. The door creaked on its hinges as they entered, and Svea graciously invited Majken into her one-room home. There was no running water, one kerosene lamp, and the only furniture was a bed, a table, a dresser, two worn chairs, and a small stove. Some old clothes hung on the wall. The woman busied herself over the stove as she made coffee. Then she began to tell about herself. Surprisingly, her voice was free of rancor.

"When I was a baby, my mother put me in a basket and placed me on someone's doorstep. Strangers raised me, and when I was fourteen I went to work in the factory. All my life I have worked in that factory. It is right over there."

She pointed out the window, brushing aside what once had been a curtain, but now was only a rag with the life scrubbed out of it.

"When I reached seventy, they said I couldn't work anymore. They gave me a small pension, and I have my little home here.

"I don't have much, Miss Broby, and I have been thinking about writing a will. But I have been praying also, and the Lord is saying, *Don't wait until you die. Give it now. Give it now . . .*"

As the words trailed off, she painfully shuffled to the dresser, opened the top drawer, and paused for a moment. She bowed her head, then turned around and slowly handed Majken an envelope.

69

"I must give it now. My life savings. Here, you must take it."

Majken reached out and hesitantly took the packet. Then she shook her head and handed the envelope back. "No, I cannot take your life savings; I cannot do that. I cannot take it."

Majken studied the wrinkles and the leathery skin on the old woman's face. She sensed the conviction of the old saint's heart and the firmness of her words as she told Majken, "Young lady, I am not giving it to *you. I am giving it to the Lord.* Never forget that."

Gently she pushed the envelope back into Majken's hands. Obediently, like a child, Majken put the packet in her purse.

Svea sat on her bed, looking very tired, but happy and relieved. "Now, that is over and done with," she said. "Now, that is done," she muttered, looking around her old room. But she was addressing a Presence beyond the physical realities of her shack.

Majken told her more of the work in Germany, but the woman seemed barely aware of her.

Shortly Majken excused herself and left the house. The last words she heard were, "God bless you; thank you for coming."

As she sat in her car, Majken opened the envelope. Tears filled her eyes as she looked inside. Two hundred, four hundred, one thousand crown. Majken wiped the tears from her eyes and drove away.

Night was settling in, and she stopped the car on the roadside. She got out and looked up at the stars. "God, I cannot count the stars, but like Abraham, I can see that they represent the number of ways that You have to take care of Your people. That is how many promises You have given us. That is how many possibilities there are to do Your will."

She got back into the car, looked again at the "widow's mite" in the envelope, and went home to tell her mother how God had answered her prayer.

The next morning, the telephone rang again. "Did you have a good night's rest, Majken?" It was the old woman.

Majken assured her that she had slept soundly and peacefully through the night. "And you . . . did you have a good night's rest?"

"No," replied the old lady in a voice quivering with emotion. "I could not sleep a wink."

*I was afraid so*, thought Majken. *I shouldn't have accepted the money. She's changed her mind.*

"Majken," the old voice went on, "I could not sleep all night. I could only walk from one side of the room to the other and then to the empty dresser drawer. All I could do was praise the Lord. I just could not imagine that my Lord could really use me to be a blessing to other people. That He would really give me, old Svea, the opportunity to be a blessing to someone. I can't tell you how happy I am."

The next week there were more gifts sent for Herr Schreiber. One woman gave some stock that a relative in the United States had purchased years ago. "I am told that it is now worthless, but you must take it and see, Majken. Maybe something can be done with it."

Majken placed the stock in her overnight bag, along with the notes from her last discussion with Herr Schreiber. They had spoken at length on what they could do after they completed the new wing. There was so much that was needed.

There was no more room to build at the present location, but several kilometers away was a piece of land that might be available. More dormitories were desperately needed if they were to empty the bunkers in Germany. Each agreed to pray about this. In a final conversation it was decided that

71

they would think about buying the land, then building six cottages, including a dispensary and a chapel.

But first, they had to pay for bricks and mortar being delivered each day for the new north wing.

With a head full of plans and an empty purse, Majken headed for Chicago.

# 8

## TESTED FAITH

Majken returned to her apartment in Chicago. Cousin Joseph arranged meetings for her during the evenings. They bought time on a Swedish radio station in Chicago, and in her native language, she told of Herr Schreiber's home for the refugees and what she had seen in Germany. She did not ask for money. She simply shared the vision and related the suffering and the needs.

Women from Joseph's church, the Philadelphia Church of Chicago, sat down with Majken and wrote letters to people whom they knew would be interested.

Little by little money began to arrive. The gifts were never in very large amounts; mostly they were one-dollar bills. But when Majken put them together at the end of each week and took them to the bank for transfer to Herr Schreiber, she did not see dollars. She saw a child, hollow-eyed, with stretched-out hands on his way to the home. She saw another empty cot in some cellar in Germany.

Majken returned to her nursing. She did not want to take any of the donated money for herself. Every penny must go to Eckernförde to buy bricks, boards, windows, paint. Each penny was the means to carry a child out of a bomb shelter and into the arms of the Sisters.

In the evenings and on weekends, she traveled from

meeting to meeting. She spent her own money for food and lodging, feeling that she dared not rob some child of a bed in the home.

One evening, well past midnight, Majken tossed and turned in her bed. She had just returned after traveling three hundred miles for a service. The weekend was over; the total offering had been thirty dollars.

As she lay, exhausted, she asked the Lord, "God, does it really pay to travel that much for thirty dollars?" The answer was quick in coming. *Majken, don't look at the money; look at the people who give it. Think of those who will receive what it can buy. You plant the seed; I will take care of the growth.*

As time progressed, Majken was to better understand this admonition. People who could give only a couple of dollars proved to be faithful over the years. It all added up to much more than the thirty dollars she received from that long weekend.

Majken was further encouraged by the cablegram from Herr Schreiber the following day. "Last brick laid, windows in, beds purchased. Social worker in Berlin assigned twenty children to occupy new building."

The news caused such celebration for Majken, her cousins, and the volunteer help that they did not consider the last words of the cable anything to worry about: "Five thousand dollars needed to pay for completion."

Several weeks later, Majken could not say where the five thousand dollars had come from, but it had come. Not that she was not a meticulous bookkeeper: Every penny was accounted for. But she noticed in the ledger that there was no one large gift. The entries were one dollar, five dollars, or ten dollars.

As Majken forwarded the last of the money to Herr Schreiber, she visualized a social worker in Berlin—maybe Frau Trebing—driving to one of those foul-smelling bunkers and pointing to a hungry little child, asking the parents if they would like their child to spend six weeks in a home on the seashore, where he would be loved, have his own bed, plenty of good food, and an opportunity to regain his health.

Majken imagined the reception that these children would receive at the home—Sister Ruth hugging each one as he arrived, hanging the threadbare sweater on a peg, and taking him into the dining room for their first meal together.

As the final payment was made on the new wing at Eckernförde, Majken was reminded of the night in Sweden after old Svea had given her life savings. She had looked up at the stars, realizing they were like the promises of God. To her they represented the number of blessings in store for those who trust with faith like that of Abraham, so well-described in Hebrews 11:12.

Majken was grateful beyond measure that at this very hour some of those "promises come true," the precious children, were settling in for their first night out of the cellars and bunkers, sliding between clean fresh sheets, washed, fed, and warm at Eckernförde.

Several days later, Majken drew out the plans that she and Herr Schreiber had discussed regarding the new piece of property. It was located just three miles from the present home. They envisioned the two becoming one mission.

Six additional buildings could be built on the new land. She had never seen the property; she only knew it overlooked the city of Eckernförde. It would be the perfect place for a home, not only for refugee children, but someday a permanent home for the motherless and fatherless: a place to take a child and lead him through the formative years, teaching him not only a trade but also moral and spiritual principles.

That day at Eckernförde—unawares to Majken—Herr Schreiber had met with the landowner. Others had also been looking at the property, but Herr Schreiber and the

Sisters laid it in prayer before the Lord. With deep assurance they later signed for the property and were given six weeks to pay for it. They had no money.

Majken was in a meeting in Tacoma, Washington, when she received a phone call from Chicago. Cousin Joseph read a telegram from Herr Schreiber: "Property today bought by faith in God. Must be paid in six weeks. Three hundred dollars needed." Majken rejoiced in the good news. She saw the hand of the Lord. The words "Before you ask, I will give . . ." ran through her mind as she convinced herself that the second part of the miracle was that it only cost three hundred dollars, an unheard-of price. She immediately sent the reply.

"Two hundred dollars in building fund. Will raise one hundred and send to you."

Back in Chicago Majken discovered her faith was to be tested further. A special message was waiting for her from Herr Schreiber. The telegram office had left off one zero. The price of the land was three *thousand*, not three hundred, dollars.

The first two hundred dollars was sent, but that still left twenty-eight hundred dollars; and the forty-five days were passing quickly. Additional money was not arriving. What was coming in was only sufficient to fill the empty beds and support new arrivals to the north wing.

Majken had planned on at least a year to raise the money for the new property. The days passed. Majken was working at her nursing job and traveling for meetings whenever she was asked.

In response to the need for someone to keep up with the bookkeeping, Clifford Claeson, an experienced bookkeeper in Chicago, had volunteered to relieve Majken of this task. Each day, Majken would call him and ask if money came in. His reply was always the same: "Nothing extra."

Majken had to admit that her faith was wavering. Determinedly she reminded herself, *God has given the plan. The property is there. Only the money is missing.*

Herr Schreiber wrote, telling how each day the children in the home gathered for prayer. He taught them that they were to take all their needs to their heavenly Father.

"Every day," wrote Herr Schreiber, "Hans, Margrette, Lothar, or Kurt asks, 'Hasn't the money come yet? We are praying for it.' "

Clifford Claeson had told Majken, "Not yet."

Majken was about to make her first trip to the west coast. She was to be in Los Angeles for several days. *Maybe*, she thought, *this is where the money will come from. There are many wealthy people in California.*

The night before the payment was due, Majken had an important service scheduled in a Los Angeles church. She was certain there was someone there who would come forward with the needed money. A friend who owned a hotel had invited her to stay there. Just before she was to leave, she was informed that there would be no meeting. The minister had forgotten about it.

"Forgotten about it!" said Majken. "How could someone forget about those pitiful children?"

Majken used the time for prayer. "God, You know that I have tried every way to get this money. You know how I have prayed. Now I just cannot do any more." Doubt oppressed her until she felt she could not rise from her knees.

Finally, she looked at her watch. Three A.M. That would make it five o'clock in Chicago. She called Mr. Claeson at his home. "No, Majken, no money yet."

Majken put the phone down, utterly defeated. Somehow she found the strength to continue praying, and her mind went back to her days as a nurse in Sweden.

As a registered nurse, she had received a monthly salary of twenty-five dollars. Most of this was used to pay back the money she had borrowed for nursing school, but at the end of five years she had managed to set aside a total of twenty-four dollars. What would she do with it? New clothes, a weekend on the seashore perhaps? Then someone had told her about a friend who was having severe financial problems and needed some money.

"How much does she need?" Majken had asked.

"Twenty dollars," had been the reply.

Majken had had no doubts. God wanted her to take her savings and give it to one in need. She had given all of her twenty-four dollars.

Now, in a strange hotel in Los Angeles, she remembered how totally happy she had been as she gave the money anonymously. The words of Jesus went through her mind: "It is more blessed to give than to receive."

Majken had scheduled a second trip to Eckernförde for when the money for the new home was raised. She had worked hard, economizing in every way possible to make another trip. Suddenly she began to see what was happening.

"But Lord," she protested, "I have already ordered my tickets. If I take that money and send it to Germany, I will not be able to go."

*If you don't get the land, you won't need to go.*

Majken got up from her bed and called Clifford Claeson. After a brief conversation, she dialed another number.

"I would like to send a cable to Eckernförde, Germany, E-C-K-E-R-N-F-O-R-D-E, Germany. Yes, that is correct, to Herr Christian Schreiber." Slowly she dictated the contents of the message. "Money wired to you today: Victory. Majken."

Later, Herr Schreiber would recount to Majken his end of the story:

There was no money, and the bank intended to sell the land to someone else at 5:30. It was 2:30 in the afternoon. What would I tell the children? A messenger delivered your telegram. I rushed to the bank for an extension and to tell them that the money was on the way. I prayed that they would accept your telegram as proof. The loan supervisor of the bank came over and shook my hand. "Congratulations, Herr Schreiber," he said. "The money just arrived from Chicago. The land is yours."

Now it was more important than ever that Majken go to Germany. But how? She had spent her savings.

Going through her dresser at home in Chicago, Majken came across the stock certificates that had been given to her in Sweden. She reread the note attached: "The Swedish government has tried for nine years to get money out of these certificates, but we are told that it is impossible. Can you do something with the papers?" Majken had to sit down when she read the last sentence. "We give the money to you for traveling expenses in your mission work."

*Is it possible?* thought Majken.

Cousin Joseph recommended a lawyer. Three lawyers told her the same thing. "The papers are too old. It is useless to try." Finally, one attorney promised that he would look into the matter. He warned Majken that there was little hope. The people who had bought the stock were dead. The papers had been inherited twice. It was extremely complicated. "I will try," he said, "but it will cost you."

Cousin Joseph and Daga joined Majken, "Casting all your care upon Him, for He careth for you" (1 Pet. 5:7). Majken read the Scripture over and over.

The day approached when the tickets must be paid for. What should she do?

When she was almost ready to cancel the trip, she received a call from the lawyer. "Please come to my office. It is about the stock."

Cousin Joseph accompanied her. The lawyer handed Majken a check. Majken gasped at the amount: twenty-four hundred dollars. It was more than enough to pay for her trip.

79

"You are very fortunate," said the lawyer. "This company went broke many years ago, but the courts are still paying investors. The time for the closure of the account is only three weeks away. Had you waited, these papers would have, indeed, been worthless."

# 9

## GAINING
## NEW SISTERS

Almost two years had passed since Majken's first trip to the cellars and bomb shelters of Germany. Now, in three weeks, Majken would travel again to New York and board a ship back to Germany.

She sat contemplating the things that had taken place and then opened the morning mail. She noticed one letter postmarked Stamford, Connecticut. She had spoken in several New England churches, but Stamford was not familiar to her. She opened the letter and began to read.

"My name is Pastor Raymond Hess. I have a small church in Stamford. Someone in our church heard you speak in Stone Church in Nyack and has strongly recommended that we ask you to speak to us. I would like to invite you to visit. Could you please let me know if you are available?"

Laying aside the rest of the mail, Majken took out a sheet of paper, stuck it in her typewriter, and hastily typed, "I am leaving Chicago to catch a boat from New York to Germany on the nineteenth of April. I have no transportation from New York, so it will be impossible to visit you at this time. I will contact you when I return from Germany, although I do not know how long I will be there."

She mailed the letter and then continued to busy herself with closing up her apartment, storing what furniture she had accumulated, and writing personal letters to those who were supporting the work.

A week passed and another letter arrived from Stamford. "If you leave on the nineteenth, then I invite you to speak at my church on the seventeenth of April. Mrs. Hess and I will pick you up in New York, take care of your luggage, and deliver you to the ship."

Moved by Pastor Hess's willingness to take care of her, Majken immediately wrote and gave her schedule. When the train arrived in New York, Pastor and Mrs. Hess were there to meet her. The warmth of that first meeting would grow and produce much fruit in the years that followed. Majken spoke at a special service at the Hesses' church. Afterwards they brought her back to New York harbor. With grateful good-byes she boarded the ship and found a place on deck amidst the streamers, the crowd, and the gay confusion. She watched the many passengers laughing and waving, their arms laden with farewell gifts. The deep blast of the ship's horn obliterated all other noise, and gracefully the ship slid away from the pier. Majken's farewell gift was standing on the dock—new friends, but more than that, fellow workers.

The welcome at Eckernförde was like a homecoming. Though she had been long absent, she was greeted as a member of the family.

Again she was met at the door by Sister Ruth. In the weeks that followed Majken gained a deeper respect for this woman, as she watched her in the day-to-day work of the home. Sister Ruth had a college education in administration, and many of the decisions concluded by Pastor Schreiber and other advisors to the home had their origins in her suggestions. She assimilated her training into a spirit of wise love and understanding that few possessed. A victim of the war herself—she never revealed what had happened to her own family—she was well-equipped to empathize with the children. Many were the times when Majken would see a frightened, withdrawn waif come into the home for the first time. Within minutes, Sister Ruth would have the child smiling, as the two walked hand-in-hand. She was a living testimony to the words that the Sisters wore on the little pin on their dress, *"Beten und Arbeiten"*—pray and work. Sister Ruth knew how to do both, and with great effectiveness.

Majken soon came to realize that each of the Sisters made a very special contribution to the work. Each was called for her particular gift.

Another such person was Sister Lydia. Somehow she seemed to have been born with the little white-edged cap sitting on her head. Majken could not imagine Sister Lydia ever being anything but a "friend of the children." Lydia, like Ruth, had an infectious smile.

Sister Lydia was a builder. Energetically she worked with physical bricks and mortar as the new buildings in the home went up, but more significantly, she was building with living stones. With a special gift of love and patience, she worked to lay a foundation in each youngster, to build the child into a trusting, hopeful adult.

One story seemed to personify the spirit of the home. Pastor Schreiber related the story to Majken without naming the Sister, as he had promised he would not.

"I received a letter from a woman who had a fine position as a supervisor in a hospital. I thought she would be a great help here, so I wrote and told her that we were starting this work but that we had no money for a salary. We could only give her a bed to sleep in and meals when the food was available.

"She requested some salary, no matter how small." As he spoke Majken speculated as to which Sister this might be.

"I told her we could give her a few marks a week, but that would be about all.

"To our surprise, she accepted the offer. Right away I could see that she was indeed a gift from God. One day she came to my office to see me. I was afraid that she was going to leave. I was greatly humbled by the time she left."

Even now Pastor Schreiber lowered his voice and looked down at his hands as he related what the Sister told him.

"She said, 'Herr Schreiber, when I see how great the need is here among the children, I feel that I have no right to accept a salary anymore.' She never accepted payment after that, but worked just as hard. Then a couple of months later she came to me again. She had no salary to give up, so I could not imagine what she wanted to tell me. I soon found out. She poured out her heart about the hardships in the home. She was not criticizing, only stating things I knew all too well. She wept as she told me how they could take care of many more children, how they would be able to give better food and care, if they only had more money.

"I agreed with her, but before I could say anything, this Sister said, 'I feel that I have no right to keep anything for myself.' With that she handed me her bankbook. 'Here,' she said, 'please use this.'"

As he finished the story, Majken realized that it could have been any one of the Sisters. On occasions when she felt alone and tired, these selfless servants caused Majken to reflect on the words of Proverbs 3:27: "Withhold not good from them to whom it is due, when it is in the power of thine hand to do it."

The new property had been acquired and paid for. But what about the buildings? It was agreed that they needed at least six cottages and a place for the Sisters to live.

There had been some discussion about selling the pigs. Though the meat provided by the annual slaughter was welcome, the animals ate enough grain to supply bread for the entire year. "Besides," agreed the Sisters, "they smell."

They butchered the pigs and remodeled the pig barn into a comfortable home for the sisters.

In another incident, a Sister came one day with something she wanted to share. She was seventy years old and had labored at the home since the first brick was set in place and the first child rescued. She had never taken wages. She received a pension of one hundred twenty marks a month and always gave half to help the home: Many times she gave her entire check. She said God had spoken to her that future homes were to be built larger, and they needed to have their faith enlarged.

A prayer meeting was held. Majken was amazed that when they finished they all had received the same message. Individually and collectively the Lord told them, *I will bless you when you put your hands to work.*

They were greatly in need of another dormitory for boys. Plans were drawn for a cinder block building to house twenty-two boys. The cost would be twenty-three thousand dollars. There was a total of two hundred twelve dollars in their building fund.

They bought two hundred dollars worth of brick and went to work. On August 5, 1955, Majken stood with a small shovel in her hands to break ground for the first building on the new property. With the children and the Sisters gathered round, Pastor Schreiber read: "But lay up for yourselves treasures in heaven, where neither moth nor rust doth corrupt, and where thieves do not break through nor steal" (Matt. 6:20).

Each day they met in prayer. They laid the blueprint on a table in the dining hall. They outlined what part they would trust the Lord for each day. The children watched and prayed with them, putting their hands on the blueprint, asking the Lord for enough cement blocks for each day's construction. Amazingly the bricks were always there before the day ended. Any skepticism harbored quickly turned to belief. Day by day, the money came in from the United States and Sweden.

There were many days when it looked dark. During those

times Majken went to her room and reminded the Lord of what she was sure He already knew. "Lord, we have no more money. We have given it all to You. We have no fund-raising organization, just a few people in the United States and Sweden. We have no influential friends. The future of these buildings and the well-being of these children are in Your hands. . . ."

Sometimes their prayers continued all through the night. There were days when the clouds never seemed to leave the skies. But slowly, Majken could see that the only darkness on the new property was the shadow cast by four walls rising cinder block by cinder block, prayer by prayer. Finally the roof was on. Then the windows were outlined in the blueprint. Two days later they were all in. Out came the paint brushes.

On May 28, 1956, the sound of hammers was replaced by singing on the hilltop overlooking the city of Eckernförde. Guests from the German government and pastors from Norway and Sweden joined children from Germany, Hungary, and Poland, the Sisters, Pastor Schreiber, and Majken in a moving dedication service. Everyone joined in singing:

> Great God we sing that mighty hand,
> By which supported still we stand.
> The opening year, thy mercy shows,
> Let mercy crown it till it close.*

Pastor Schreiber read from Psalm 118: "This is the day which the Lord hath made; we will rejoice and be glad in it." It was, indeed, a day to be joyful.

---

* "Great God We Sing That Mighty Hand" *Trinity Hymnal* (Philadelphia: The Orthodox Presbyterian Press,) p. 612.

# *10*

# LITTLE CHILDREN HURT TOO

As the days passed, Majken found her perspective on the home changing. She was writing more letters, working with Herr Schreiber and Sister Ruth with more concern and a greater zeal. More plans for additional dormitories were formulated. But above all, she was cherishing the time she spent with the children. She could challenge every person in the world to support the work; she could have vaults filled with money, but if the lives of these children were not transformed into the likeness of Jesus Christ, then the ministry was a failure. Quietly, patiently, at the dinner table, at the side of the play yard, sitting on the edge of the bed at night in a darkened room, she listened to them as they tried to talk away the past.

These children were only a few of the thousands who still needed help. Their backgrounds varied, but their experiences were much the same. They were precious souls whose lives were marred with tragedy. They needed love and care.

There was thirteen-year-old Helmut. He had no idea where his mother and father were. They might both be dead or in a prison camp. They had been separated while attempting to escape, and he had been passed from relative to relative in camp after camp.

Majken was assisting in the infirmary when Helmut was given his physical by Dr. Arnold Wicke. Wicke was the director of the district health department. Several times a week, he came from Eckernförde to examine the children. But he was more than a physician. As he examined eyes and ears, thumped backs, and applied his stethoscope, he subtly observed what was coming from the soul of the child. His recommendations were highly valued by the Sisters in understanding and treating the physical and spiritual needs of the children.

Gently but deftly Dr. Wicke checked Helmut's arms and legs for bruises, abnormalities in his skin, fractures or chips in the bones that might have gone unnoticed. Then he pulled out his rubber hammer and lightly tapped Helmut's knee. "Good, good," he murmured kindly. "Your father, I'll bet he is proud of a young boy like you?"

There was silence as Dr. Wicke continued to tap Helmut's knee. Finally the boy spoke. "He is gone."

"Gone?" Dr. Wicke asked as he began to peer into Helmut's ears through his instrument.

The boy was silent, and Dr. Wicke moved on to Helmut's eyes. "Maybe someday he will be back."

Silence.

"Your mother must be a very handsome woman to bring such a fine specimen like yourself into the world," Dr. Wicke continued evenly.

More silence, and then pressing his lips together Helmut answered, "She is gone too . . . they are both gone."

"Gone is a big place," said Dr. Wicke.

"Yes, it is a big place."

"Maybe someday . . ." said Dr. Wicke.

"No," said Helmut.

The finality of his reply stabbed at Majken's heart. *But, maybe there is hope,* she almost cried aloud. *Perhaps they are not dead, only lost.* Her own heart begged for more. What the child did not dare to hope, she would hope for him. A tear trickled down her cheek and quickly she brushed it away.

More questions; a few, hesitant answers. Little by little, Helmut told what he remembered of his mother and father and the last time he had seen them. Subtly, unobtrusively, Dr. Wicke drew out the examination until the full story lay before him.

He stood and looked at Helmut. His black, unruly hair needed cutting. His brown eyes lacked sparkle and life, and his pale, skinny body cried for proper food and rest; but more important, his spirit needed to be nourished with hope and love.

"The Sisters will make you healthy in no time," said Dr. Wicke as he stepped back and began to put his instruments in his bag.

Helmut sat on the examining table and waited for Dr. Wicke to look up. He stared straight into the physician's eyes.

"Doctor," he said solemnly, speaking precisely but without expression, "you and the others can try to make me happy, but there is one thing you can never do." He paused for a moment, his face like granite. "I will never laugh again in this life."

As Helmut slid off the examining table, Majken thought back to her time at the border. She remembered a mother who told her that she had lost her little boy. All she had was a very old picture taken when he was very small. The mother was standing outside a bunker staring at a huge bulletin board. It was covered with large posters with the headlines, "These children are seeking their parents." Below were various pictures captioned "name unknown" or "first name unknown."

Across the faces of several pictures were stamped in large letters, "This boy found." It was the dream of every parent to see that stamp across the face of his or her child. The woman showed her photograph to Majken. "Have you seen him? He is now fifteen years old." Majken studied the picture, then returned it to the woman, unable to speak. She could only shake her head no. The woman smoothed the torn edges of the picture carefully, slipped it back into the pocket of her ragged coat, and walked away.

*Helmut is one of those children,* thought Majken. Neither she nor Dr. Wicke spoke; what the boy had said had shaken them both.

Then there was Franz, who looked a little like Helmut, except Franz had hope written all over his face. He was very shy and reticent, but when he did speak, a bright smile spread across his thin, pasty face, tightly drawn over high cheekbones. He had never heard about God, but he did know that his mother was alive and seeking a home for him. How long this would take, no one knew. Sometimes it took months, sometimes years. Franz sat in the daily Bible class and hungrily stored away every word. His expression was always just a small movement away from what Majken sensed was the joy of complete understanding.

When Dr. Wicke was examining Franz, he asked, "Well, Franz, what are your plans for the future?"

Without a moment's hesitation, with all the solemn certainty that a man of twelve years could muster, he replied, "Doctor, I want to become a minister."

As Majken was drawn to Helmut, so she was equally drawn to Franz. Though the boys had totally different personalities, she saw the potential, but also the needs, of each.

Then there was Rheinhard.

Rheinhard resembled neither Helmut nor Franz. He was blonde with deep-set blue eyes—eyes that continually roved Majken's face when she talked to him. He brought with him a brief from the social worker in Berlin. It was not pleasant reading.

At age three, his father was killed while in the army. His

mother fled with Rheinhard to the west of Germany. After escaping, she remembered some precious momentos her husband had given to her before he left. It was all she had to remember him by. Leaving the boy with friends, she returned to her old home, where she was captured by Communist police. It was believed she was sent to a prison in Siberia. Rheinhard was shuffled from one refugee camp to another. He was the youngest of the children who had arrived at Eckernförde. His body was small and frail. His face looked like that of a twelve-year-old, and he acted more adult than some of the boys that age. Majken could not believe it when she read the entry: *Present age: 6 years.*

*Impossible,* she thought. Dr. Wicke looked over the papers, and examined the boy. He agreed with the social worker. Further investigation indicated that Rheinhard was indeed six years old.

Helmut, the boy who would never smile on this earth; Franz, who wanted to become a minister; and Rheinhard, who only wanted his mother; were a microcosm of the hundreds of thousands of children adrift in the Western world.

Day after day, Majken, the Sisters, and Pastor Schreiber were the hands that cradled, comforted, and fed. The needs were so great. The challenge: to instill a measure of hope into their hearts while working to block out the painful past.

With the first new house in operation, Majken made another trip to the refugee camps. It was as if she had never been there before. Gone forever was the possibility that she might erase from her mind the horror of the first trip, shoving what she had seen back in the recesses of her subconscious as a nightmare to be forgotten.

The stench, the hollow eyes, the desperate parents, the lethargic children: The tragic plight of these innocent victims of man's inhumanity to man haunted her. This time she noticed more than before the plight of the young girls.

When she returned to Eckernförde, she knew that plans for a second building on the new property would have to be accelerated. No matter what the cost, they must build a cottage for girls as they had already done for the boys.

She devised a way to rearrange the beds so that a building the same size as the boys' dormitory could accommodate twenty-four girls, four more than in the first dormitory. Pastor Schreiber, Sister Ruth, and the rest laid their request before the Lord, and Pastor Schreiber had blueprints drawn. Inflation had hit Germany. In the thirteen months that had passed since the opening of the boys' dormitory, the price of building materials had doubled. The cost would be fifty-eight thousand dollars.

"Well," said Sister Ruth, "we will just have to pray twice as hard." The new need would have to be filled after the daily costs of feeding the one hundred and twenty children already being cared for. There had been no new money promised nor pledges made, and there was no loan available. Once again the need would have to be made known. Little by little the money would come in. Meanwhile, they all prayed much and believed God was hearing.

Once again there were days when all the food was gone. Majken never stopped marveling that no one ever missed a meal.

Majken increased her letter-writing, telling people of what was being done. She wrote about the children, those who were in the home and those still in the cellars, the bunkers, and on the streets.

Busily she made plans for the summer of 1957: another trip to America to extend her hand to more people. But instead of boarding an airplane for America, she found herself in the hospital with a severe liver infection.

Majken lay in the hospital bed, unable to move. Long periods of nausea swept over her body. Each day one of the Sisters came to visit. When she asked how much money

92

was coming in for the second dormitory, they simply told her to rest. Majken knew what that meant. Desperately she cried out to the Lord on behalf of pathetic little ones who needed the home. They had to be reached before TB, anemia, and other diseases destroyed their bodies. They had to be rescued before they lost the desire to live, before their youthful hope was drowned in adolescent bitterness.

The largest gift that had ever been received was three hundred dollars, and now they needed twenty-four hundred dollars within two weeks' time. They would have to inform the social worker that they couldn't take in any more girls. How tragic! The thought alone was more than Majken's frail body could stand.

She lay in the hospital for thirty-two days, too weak to write of the needs of the home or her own ill health. Only the staff realized how critical the situation was. Finally, as she continued to weaken, able to expend her energies only in prayer, Majken resigned herself to the Lord. "Father, I know that as far as humans are concerned this is impossible. But somewhere in the world tonight there is one person upon whom You will lay the burden of twenty-four hundred dollars. The children must be rescued. You love them more than we do."

Two days later, Majken was much improved—so much so that she was taken back to the home. She did not expect any money until the first of August, since Mr. Claeson sent the money that came into the American office on the first of each month. The deadline could not be met. But at noon, July 26, the mail came. A letter was brought to her postmarked Chicago. Excitedly she ripped it open. She began to weep as she read, "Dear Majken, I feel strangely moved to send you this check right away. It has just come in the mail." Through tear-filled eyes, Majken looked at the check. It was for exactly twenty-four hundred dollars.

Several months later, while in the United States, Majken

learned these details. At the same time that Majken was asking the Lord to move upon the heart of someone who had twenty-four hundred dollars, on a farm in western Canada, almost a world away, an old farmer could not sleep. He had been reading a magazine called the *Herald of Faith*. It was a small four-page magazine published by Majken's Cousin Joseph in Chicago. Each month Majken wrote a small article about her work.

Impatiently the old man waited for morning to arrive. Then he arose, dressed, and drove a short distance to the home of his daughter and son-in-law. He told them that he had to go to town.

"Why, Father? It is still early in the morning."

The old man held up the magazine and pointed to Majken's article. "This lady, this Majken what's-her-name, she needs help. God is speaking to me, and I must go to town and send some money to this place in Germany . . . this place, Eckernförde."

The old man's children knew their father's closeness to God too well to argue. They drove him to town and waited until the bank opened. He was first in line. Speedily he had the money withdrawn and indicated the address in Germany where he wished it sent.

"You don't send this kind of money to Germany from this bank," protested the bank officer." We have no facilities for such a transaction. You must go to a larger bank. I can try to do it for you here, but it will take at least a month."

"No," the old man argued, "that money is needed right now."

The banker looked at the address. He also noted that there was a Chicago address given for people living in the United States.

A few minutes later, the old man, his daughter, and his son-in-law went to the post office and mailed the bank draft, special delivery, to Chicago.

# 11

# GOD LOVES
# CHILDREN

On a cool autumn day in 1957 the Eckernförde sky was crisp and clear. City officials, church leaders, Pastor Schreiber, Majken, the staff, and one hundred twenty children from the cellars and bomb shelters of Europe filled the air with music. To Majken it was an offering to the Lord, as much as any ever given by a high priest.

> A mighty fortress is our God,
> A bulwark never failing,
> Our helper He, amid the flood
> Of mortal ills prevailing.

Another dedication service and reception for the twenty-four girls was taking place.

Especially anxious for the girls to arrive was Sister Ella. She had already moved into the dormitory and was ready to be a mother to all of them. No one doubted that she would do anything less. Since the early days of the home, whenever a child needed someone special, Ella was there. She could be heard praying long into the night for her children, each by name and need. When they suffered, she suffered; when they cried, she cried; when they laughed, she laughed.

Now she surveyed her new troupe of charges. All were in need of new clothes, a bath, and a hairbrush; but more than that, they needed love. In minutes, Sister Ella was moving among them, patting a shoulder here, hugging a frightened little one there, buttoning up dresses, and pouring out gentle concern.

The oldest of the girls was Elise. She was fifteen; like the rest she looked younger physically, but old, so old in her countenance. She had attempted to commit suicide five times.

There was Frieda; small, very thin, nine years old, hanging on tightly to her older sister, Gerda. Gerda was not much bigger, although she was two years older.

Ella went over to them. Frieda smiled, but Gerda turned away. "Just leave me alone. I don't want to talk."

The last time someone had tried to speak to Gerda with any compassion in her voice was a couple of months earlier, as both of the girls stood by the casket of their mother. The social worker had warned the Sisters that Gerda might be a serious problem.

There was little Gretchen, who was recovering from tuberculosis. Her body still showed the effects of murine typhus. She had been cross-eyed since birth. She wore a pair of boy's trousers, full of holes, and was barefoot. At six years of age, she looked like a creature that had been dropped by the side of the road and left for dead.

When she had arrived at the home, Sister Lydia had sat her down and asked her name. Sister Ella had to ask her several times. They finally decided she was mumbling "Gretchen." Lydia began to write her name down and Gretchen became wild, yelling, scratching, and trying to escape. She finally collapsed on the floor in a heap, crying, but too tired to resist. As Sister Ella tried to lead her to her bed, she again looked around wildly, her body cowering like a cornered animal.

The original children's home in Eckernförde, Germany, was destroyed by fire in 1958.

Herr Schreiber is seen here instructing the boys at Eckernförde in carpentry and woodworking.

In 1961, Majken visited Berlin, where scenes like this one were common. The building stands in East Berlin, the sidewalk in West Berlin. As the wall dividing the city was being raised, many people fled to freedom.

The Berlin Wall, erected in 1961, drastically reduced the number of new refugees into West Germany.

Seven hundred people, three hundred of them children, lived in this windowless bunker in Braunschweig, Germany, during the 1950s.

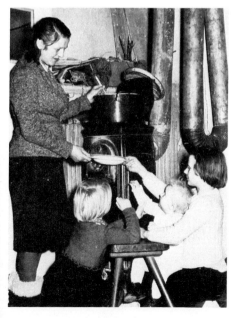

Inside the bunkers, families made do with cramped living quarters and meager food supplies.

On a hill overlooking the Baltic Sea, another cottage was built following this groundbreaking ceremony at Eckernförde.

This building, built in 1957, is representative of the living quarters and grounds at Eckernförde today.

The *Haven of Rest* radio broadcast raised funds for this chapel at Eckernförde, built in 1966.

After months of digging, Herr Schreiber and his Moroccan coworkers finally hit water, a precious resource for these people of the Sahara Desert.

This mother and baby daughter wait outside the new medical clinic at BouRbia Two.

Automobile travel in the Sahara is risky business, as Majken often discovered. Here, her loaded station wagon was again stuck in the sand.

When left without wheels, Majken opted for a more dependable—but much slower—form of transportation when making her medical rounds to nearby oases.

Having heard of her need for quicker and more reliable transportation, the National Association of Christian Congregational Churches presented Majken and daughter Christine with a new Jeep Land Rover for the Sahara work.

After Hurricane Fifi rampaged across Honduras, fifteen hundred people moved to a small plot of land and established homes like the one pictured here.

A multipurpose building, built through the fund-raising efforts of the *Haven of Rest* ministry, provides facilities to serve two hundred Honduran children one meal per day.

After nine months of training, these Honduran women graduated as qualified seamstresses, a skill that could help them provide for their families.

"You wrote my name in a big book."

"Yes," said Sister Ella, "so we will know who you are."

Gretchen ducked her head with a shivering sigh. Sister Ella could barely catch the words as she spoke in a very low whisper. "When you write a person's name in a big book then they are either dead, or they are going to go away. And I don't want to go away again."

Later at the dinner table, after she gained some confidence, she asked Sister Ella, "Who has been able to steal so much food? How many beggars do you have that they can beg so much?"

The twenty-four girls had barely settled into their new home when Majken began to ask the Lord, "What next? Where do we go from here?"

Guidance came in the form of an update on the refugee situation provided by a social worker in Berlin. Majken fluctuated between indignation and pity as she read the letter.

In the last eleven months, 160,000 new refugees have come into West Germany. They join the 13,400,000 who are already here. They are walking the streets, living in backyards, cellars, and the bomb shelters that you visited. Though our government is working as hard as they can to find jobs and homes, the people keep coming faster than we can take care of them.

We think that we are just getting ahead of the mass influx, when the Communists initiate another purge, and again we are overwhelmed by wailing people, running for their lives. As you saw when you were here, they do not bring much with them, and many families are separated in the exodus.

It is as though the Soviet Union knows our plight and is deliberately flooding us with refugees. The Communists must do all they can to keep the economy of West Germany from recovering.

Majken visualized the hundreds of refugees running for their lives, anxiety mingled with hope. In her mind's eye she could see them collapsing into each other's arms when they reached freedom at last, daring to believe that life would be different. But she knew how quickly the great expectations turned to hopelessness.

Majken held the report on her lap and began to pray and weep. She rejoiced in the mercy of the Lord from the past three years, but still she remembered the children and the open land where more buildings could be constructed. A poem came to her mind which she had memorized years before. She could not remember the author or even why she had learned it, but the words came back to her, clear and complete. She folded her hands on her lap and recited aloud:

> Millions have perished
>     in war and terror . . .
>         we survive.
> Millions are homeless,
>     we are sheltered.
> This night in all the world,
>     for every man well nourished,
>         three are hungry . . . we are fed.
> The world's substance
>     should have blessed mankind
>         with homes, health, and competence.
> Instead it has been used
>     to destroy all these,
>         to breed pestilence, misery, and poverty.
> Each life is tested
>     by its answer to the question
>         first asked in the world's beginning:
> "Am I my brother's keeper?"

Majken knew the answer. "Yes, I am my brother's keeper."

There was no one to hear her, but she made a vow. "We are sheltered: we are fed. I don't know why. But as my brother's keeper, I must go to those who are sheltered, who are not hungry, who have bread to eat, who have homes to sleep in, and tell them that there are millions who are not so fortunate. And then I must ask them, will you help? I must stretch out my hand in the name of Jesus on behalf of those whose hands are trembling from malnutrition, fear, and uncertainty."

Two weeks later, Majken was back in the United States. Now that she was an American citizen she no longer had to be concerned with matters of immigration, so she immediately went to work contacting people who were interested in the home.

She told Cousin Joseph and Daga of the new plans. There would be another new dormitory. Before she left Germany, Pastor Schreiber, the Sisters, and Majken all agreed that it was time to add building number three to their master plan.

But this time, Majken's trip was different. There was a new kind of challenge for her. Everyone in America was so busy with their own lives that the tragedy of the refugees was either forgotten or lost in the political rhetoric of a divided Germany. People seemed more interested in arguing whether General Eisenhower was right in allowing the Soviet Union half of Berlin, or whether the United States should have taken it all. Little was mentioned about the human suffering.

Majken would need much prayer.

# 12

## TESTED BY FIRE

It took three weeks to put together an itinerary. She decided to begin in Florida and cross America, including Canada, returning to Chicago, and ending up in Connecticut. It was the first of seven such trips that Majken would make in as many years.

She had little money, and she was especially concerned about having to spend money on food, lodging, and gas. She had purchased a used car that she was skeptically optimistic would make the trip, but she was concerned about having to take money to buy a tank of gas.

Every time she pulled up to a gas station and spent four dollars to fill the tank, she calculated how many cinder blocks that same amount of money would buy or how many meals it would have provided for the children.

When she arrived at a town, she searched out a cheap motel, freshened up, and then located the church or home where the meeting was to be held.

Most of the churches she visited were very small. Sometimes she was asked to speak briefly on Sunday morning, but more often she was relegated to a Wednesday night service or a special Women's Missionary Society meeting in a private home.

So often the pastor said, "I am sorry for such a small

turnout, but you just happen to be here when the circus is in town," or "We just finished our missions conference." There was always an apology.

It never disturbed Majken that only a few people came to meet her. She was convinced: Just as it was a small, dedicated minority in the Soviet Union causing this nightmare for so many millions of people, it would also be a small, dedicated minority who would meet that satanic challenge and in the end cause the Communists to fail.

Majken was looking forward to her time in Florida. When she had visited in 1953, she had stayed in the home of Mrs. Elma Cook. From time to time, Mrs. Cook had sent in monthly gifts for the work. She was not wealthy, but her interest in Majken's work sparked a special friendship.

Majken had promised Mrs. Cook that when she returned she would stay at her home. Majken arrived late one afternoon. She was hot and very tired, her clothes wrinkled and her hair disheveled. Mrs. Cook prepared a quick meal and insisted that Majken take a nap.

There was an evening meeting scheduled at the small church where Mrs. Cook attended. The interest was encouraging, but the offering was small. It was a pattern that Majken was already used to. She never counted the money as a one-time gift. She had already learned that not only did people give regularly after they gave the first time, but their interest increased as giving progressed.

The next morning was free for Majken to rest. Early in the afternoon, Mrs. Cook asked Majken to go shopping with her. They arrived at a department store, and Mrs. Cook insisted that Majken try on several rather expensive dresses. They cost more than Majken had ever spent for clothes before, but she had to admit they felt very good.

Under vigorous protest from Majken, Mrs. Cook told the salesclerk to wrap up all of the dresses that Majken had tried on.

On the way home, Mrs. Cook explained. "I think it is important that as an ambassador of Jesus Christ you be neat, modest, and well-dressed."

When Majken got home, she compared her new wardrobe with the dresses she had brought from Chicago. She had to admit that her old clothes were quite seedy-looking. She held up the dress that she had worn to the meeting the night before. *She's right,* she told herself, *it makes me look like an old maid.*

After an evening of rest, Majken had her strength back and was ready for the second leg of her trip. She was dressed in an attractive new dress, which Mrs. Cook pronounced "sufficient."

Just before leaving, Mrs. Cook began to talk to Majken in a very motherly way.

"Majken, I don't think it is right that you work as hard as you do to raise money for those children in Germany and then have to spend it on gas and food and motels."

"Yes," said Majken, "I have been praying about that."

Mrs. Cook reached into a drawer and pulled out an envelope. She handed it to Majken.

"I want you to use these. It is my part in helping these children."

Majken looked at Mrs. Cook and then opened the envelope. She reached in and took out four credit cards.

"Use them," said Mrs. Cook simply.

They had a short prayer together, and Majken began her journey to California with a deeper assurance of the Father's care. Until Elma Cook's death in 1963, Majken never had to take anything from her offerings to pay for her expenses in America.

As one motel sign faded into another, Majken continued her trek across the United States. Often she wished that she had someone who could travel with her. Often she thought about how nice it would be to have a child of her own, who could be a traveling companion.

The days stretched out to two months. Every evening was the same. She came back from a meeting, counted the offering, and put it in a safe place so that in the morning she could stop at a post office, purchase a money order, and send the funds to Chicago.

One night she lay down on her bed in another motel, in another city, too tired to count the meager offering. "There truly must have been a circus in town," she said with a rueful smile as she looked at the few one-dollar bills. She would count it in the morning. She ached so badly that she could hardly breathe. There was a note pad by the telephone. After a moment's reflection she picked it up and scribbled instructions as to whom to notify if she should be found dead. Her system was so depleted, she was not sure that she would ever wake up.

Nine hours later she awakened. She read the note and then tore it up. She realized for the first time just how tired she really was. It was no longer safe to be driving alone. She made a few phone calls and headed for Cousin Joseph's.

After several days of Daga's special care, Majken had regained her strength and immediately grew restless.

February is always cold in Chicago, but 1958 seemed to be especially so. Majken began to spend time in cities surrounding Chicago. At times life seemed to be one continuous blizzard.

February 3 was one of those days. Majken had spent four hours making the trip to a small church in Zion, Illinois. It was a trip that ordinarily would not have taken more than an hour.

It was a "good" meeting. The people were interested and some of them gave more than they could afford. She was feeling better as she guided her car through the snow. But soon the wind rose until she could see only a couple of feet in front of her. It was well after midnight when she pulled into Cousin Joseph's driveway. Wearily she rested her forehead on the steering wheel and silently thanked the Lord for guiding her home safely.

Then she opened the car door, bracing herself against the cold blast of wind. She was surprised to see that all the lights in the house were on. No matter how late, Cousin Daga always had a warm fire and low lights waiting in Majken's bedroom, but tonight even the porch light glared through the drifting snow.

Before she could get her key into the lock Cousin Daga opened the door. "Come in, you must be freezing to death."

She helped her with her coat, brushing away the snow briskly, then hurried off to the kitchen. "I have some hot tea and toast waiting," she said over her shoulder.

Majken slowly pulled off her boots and set them beside the door. She knew that something was wrong. Cousin Joseph was traveling. Had he died? Was it Mother?

Daga came into the living room and settled a small, enameled tray on a table in front of Majken's chair. Majken gratefully took a piece of toast and poured her tea, as Cousin Daga took an armchair a few feet away. They sat quietly for a few moments, then Daga said gently, "Majken, can you take some bad news?"

"Is it Mother?" she asked anxiously, setting aside her teacup and saucer.

Daga shook her head. "No, Sigrid is fine. It's the home."

Daga handed Majken a piece of paper. "This arrived early this evening from Germany."

Majken unfolded the telegram hesitantly.

"Today house on hill burned. All food and clothing lost. Praise God, no one injured."

Majken stared at the paper in disbelief.

"That is where we had all our food and clothing stored. There will be no food, no clothing, and it's winter."

Softly Daga crossed the room and put her arm around her

cousin. "But, Majken, no one was injured. Food and clothing, they can be replaced." She knelt before her, taking her hand. "Come, let us pray. Let us thank the Lord that no one was injured."

Majken slid to her knees obediently. Suddenly the blizzard that she had just conquered seemed so insignificant. "Remember, Majken," said Daga in her quiet, gentle way, "we gave that building to Jesus. It is His building that burned down, not ours."

Majken felt a surge of anger. *Why, Lord, why?* The words of old Svea echoed in her head, "Remember, I am not giving the money to you, young lady. I am giving it to the Lord."

Humbled anew, Majken joined Daga in her thanksgiving. Gone was the desire to question, to argue. Instead Majken was at peace. Joyfully she laid aside her petitions and focused on praising God for what He had already done.

Renewed in spirit, Majken moved back to her chair as Daga went to make a fresh pot of tea. Later, they sat talking together on how wonderfully the Lord had supplied all of their needs. Together they reminded each other (as though it were necessary) how God had provided the stock to be used at just the right time; how the old man in Canada had been burdened in the middle of the night to send the money that had bought the new property.

The wind was still, the snowy world smooth and white as daylight crept through the windows. Majken took a last sip of cold tea. "What," she asked Daga, "do you suppose the Lord will bring out of this?"

"I do not know," answered Daga frankly, "but remember, He owns the cattle on a thousand hills. Only one of his storehouses burned. He has many more."

In Eckernförde, Pastor Schreiber, the Sisters, and the children stood before the pile of rubble that only hours before had been their food supply and their clothing.

# MAJKEN

The word *why?* was on Pastor Schreiber's lips when one of the younger boys walked up. He took the man's hands, and for the first time since the tragedy, a prayer was uttered.

"Dear God," said the boy, in a small, quiet voice, "You can do everything. You can rebuild that house." He paused for a moment and then added confidently, "And I know that You will."

Pastor Schreiber looked over the half-frozen, impressionable faces before him. "Out of ashes will come something beautiful. Father," he prayed, "give me the faith of this little child."

Seven months passed. August 28, 1958. Majken stood in Eckernförde, Germany, amazed at the beauty that the Lord had brought out of ashes. Instead of a burned-out frame, there was a beautiful building; but more important, the building housed twenty homeless boys and girls. Majken had just helped to tuck each one into bed. As she prayed with them, she promised that tomorrow there would be food on the table, clothes to wear, and that they would not have to leave.

Majken walked over to the side of the building and lovingly touched the wreath of flowers from the dedication earlier in the day. Gazing at the sea, she recalled the ceremony. The Mayor of Eckernförde had been there, other government officials, and also the Governor of Schleswig-Holstein. She thought of the witness the building was to those who needed Christ as much as the children.

In his speech the governor said, "We are proud that this home is in our district. Ten years ago the condition here was such that as far as we could see it was impossible to build anything. I am happy to know that this children's home is built on the old Christian foundation.

"Because of this the atmosphere is such that young people and children who are given care can one day be of great value to our country and to the whole world."

The owner of the estate who had sold the land for the home, Count Felix von Bethman-Holweg, stepped to the podium. Majken could see that his noble features were moved by what the Lord had done on a piece of land he once had deemed useless. There was no regret in his voice as he spoke.

"When Pastor Schreiber came to me and wanted to build a home for children, I thought that it could not be done. We counted only with the material things because there was famine in the country. Money had no value. There were no building materials to be found, no bricks, no cement, no wood, no nails. Here he came with a few broken parts of a barracks and said he wanted to build a home for children— for refugee children.

"The district was under English occupation. No German was permitted to sell or rent property. The entire plan seemed impossible. But I went to the English governor who had taken over my castle. He made an exception.

"And now, history has repeated itself. Again God has done the impossible. A new house stands where the burned-out one was before. It is no longer full of food and clothing. It houses twenty boys and girls, all under the age of twelve."

There was no doubt in Majken's mind that God would work in the lives of those twenty newcomers, as He had worked so many times before. Humbly she prayed, "Lord, we don't know much about these little ones yet, except that they need Your love. Make us worthy vessels." As she walked the grounds, Majken thought of the other children who had spent time at Eckernförde.

She remembered Ulf. He was eleven when he came to live with them. Gradually, as they prayed and talked with him, they discovered how terrible his experiences had been. Ulf's father, whom he loved very much and who represented strength and security to Ulf, died very suddenly. Ulf was not able to accept the loss, and he became very aggressive and bitter. He ran away from his mother, who was sick and frail, and joined forces with a gang of boys bent on theft and violence. He could not be kept in any school.

When Ulf arrived at the home he was confused and angry. It took all the love and patience that the Sisters could muster to keep him there. Then one Sunday morning, Ulf was heard praying in the chapel service. A noticeable change came over him. The children were encouraged to write one letter a week to relatives or friends, and suddenly Ulf asked for help in writing to his mother. Majken read the result:

Dear Mother,
I am so sorry for all the trouble that I have given you. I have not been good. Forgive me.
I enclose a handkerchief in this letter so that you can dry all the tears that I have caused you to cry when I have been bad toward you.
I will try to become a better boy because I love you.
Your Ulf

Ulf gave Majken a clean handkerchief, his only one, to put in the letter, and then waited anxiously for the response.

Two weeks later, Ulf's letter came back. The handkerchief was still inside untouched. A note was attached. "Ulf's mother died three weeks ago by her own hand. She has been buried."

At first Ulf wept as he read the note. Then he quietly took the handkerchief in his hand and wiped his tears away. He stopped talking to the Sisters and neither cried nor smiled.

Two weeks went by and then one night, Ulf did not show up for dinner. The home was searched. Ulf could not be found. Pastor Schreiber went into town looking for him. Several of the Sisters walked to some of the homes in the area in search of him.

Late in the evening he was found. He was at a railroad station eighteen miles away. Tired, hungry, and sobbing uncontrollably, Ulf told the Sisters that all he wanted to do was to see his mother's grave. He wanted to give her the handkerchief. He didn't want her to cry anymore.

The trip was arranged. Ulf visited his mother's grave and saw the room where she had died.

Majken looked at the darkened windows of the first home built on the new property. In that dormitory, sleeping soundly was one of the finest boys in the home. He had compassion when others lost their patience. He displayed a great amount of love for his younger brothers when they were sad. He was quick to testify as to how Jesus Christ had changed his life.

"I used to want to run away from the home, but now I want to stay." Ulf had become a new person.

"Dear Lord, I am sure there are some Ulfs in that new home. Thank you that you have sent them to us." Eyes flooded with tears, Majken turned and began to make her way to her own room. She thought of the people who had helped to rebuild the home. She knew few names, but she would not forget the faces. Vividly she saw the firemen who had worked to save the first building come back to lay new cinder blocks on the ruins. She saw the truck coming into the driveway with the lumber donated by a friend in Sweden. She saw the letter from someone in the United States who said, "I just heard about the fire. Here is all I have. Please use it."

She thought of the quick trip to Sweden that she had made. She had been invited to speak at a couple of churches. They were just small churches, attended by only a handful of people. But they were God's people, and Majken never turned from the opportunity to spend precious time with them.

She remembered another series of incidents. One spring morning, while studying her Bible and praying, she realized the need for woolen blankets for the coming winter. There were no blankets for the new house to be dedicated in a few months, and the other eighty beds needed new blankets as well. Later in the day she visited a blanket factory in town. She had neither money nor promise of money to come. But when she left the factory, she had in hand an order for one hundred woolen blankets, to be delivered in sixty days.

Later in the evening, she began to worry. Had she extended faith too far? By morning she was reassured: God would supply.

She had been invited for breakfast in the home of a woman she had never met. During their conversation Majken told how the Lord had built the home and mentioned the blankets she had ordered for the children. Nothing more was said.

It was August before Majken heard from the woman again. "I just couldn't get away from thinking about the blankets," she wrote. "I just felt that I had to do something about them. I rode my bicycle to all the farms here and asked the people to donate money for the blankets. I am sending you the bankbook of the account where I have deposited the money."

*Tonight*, thought Majken, *because a seventy-year-old lady urged on by the Lord cycled around the countryside, we have one hundred new blankets, keeping one hundred children warm. "He is able to give more than we ask"—there was enough money left over to buy furniture for the new home.*

*Lord, thank You, not only for the children, but for those who are colaborers, those who follow Your leading, and fulfill Your work. Only You can bring such beauty out of ashes.*

# 13

# A LITTLE
# BOY'S FAITH

Majken sat in her room and thumbed through her diary. Three months had passed since the third house had been raised out of the ashes. She read again what she had written the previous week:

> November 1, 1958. Five years have passed since God called me to work among the refugee children in Europe. God opened to us the work in Eckernförde and inspired us to build, trusting only in Him.
>
> Just now there is a darkness when it comes to finances. Last Tuesday we made a promise to accept twenty more children. These are not only refugees, but problem children. They have been in trouble with the police or their parents cannot handle them. We will keep these children until they are old enough to care for themselves.
>
> Each bed is full and our cupboards are bare several times a week. We live from day to day. If we say no what will happen to them? The words are ringing in my ears from John 11:40, "If thou wouldest believe, thou shouldest see the glory of God." It is with fear and trembling but with confidence that we have done the right thing, that we now accept the children. We must start to build the fourth house, along with the chapel and clinic.

Any feeling of failure that Majken might have experienced in reading that entry was erased by the next lines.

November 11. Wonderful revival among our teen-agers. The Spirit of God is moving on their hearts and many of our problem youngsters have accepted Jesus Christ as their Savior.

She read on.

November 15, 1958. Lord, we are waiting for help. The children must be cared for. Income today is twelve dollars. We thank You, Lord, for this. Bless the people who gave; but help us through.

For a few moments she forgot about the physical needs, as she read the next day's entry:

Today was one of those sad and happy days. We saw the reason for our existence, but at the same time we were saddened. Franz, once so shy he would hardly talk to anyone, is now a different boy. Sister Ruth heard him pray in chapel, "Dear Jesus, will You make my black heart white and write my name in the Lamb's Book of Life?" He will tell anyone who will listen that he is going to be a minister like Herr Schreiber. His health at first was very precarious, but now it is much better, for which we are most thankful.

Today Franz left us. That in itself is good news. His mother is now in a position to keep him herself; she has found a job and a home. But the farewells were tinged with sadness. There were many tears as we said good-bye to Franz. His last words to us were to remember that Jesus had made his black heart white, and that he would come back someday as a minister.

Majken put her diary down and thought not only of Franz, but of Rheinhard and Helmut, the other two boys who had arrived at the home the same day. She wished that Helmut had made as much progress. His brown hair was darker now; his shoulders broader and his frame taller as he approached young manhood. But still written across his face were the words that he had spoken three years before to Dr. Wicke, "You can try to make me happy, but there is

112

one thing that you can never do. I will never laugh again in this life."

As Rheinhard had grown over the past three years, he had come to show an active interest in other people, but the Sisters could sense that still he was preoccupied. There was something deep inside Rheinhard that was struggling to find expression. One day he came to Sister Lydia after the daily Bible class that Herr Schreiber taught.

"Sister Lydia," he asked, "can I really pray for anything I want?"

"Why, yes, anything," said Lydia, expecting the conversation to be dropped at that point. But Rheinhard continued. "Sister Lydia, if I pray for anything, will God answer my prayer?"

Lydia realized that this was not just a child's inquiry. She hesitated for a moment, and then replied, "Yes, Rheinhard, that is what Jesus said."

The boy stared at Lydia for a few moments; then in a quiet, resolute voice, he said, "Then I shall ask that the Lord Jesus bring my mother back."

Lydia stared at him for a moment, wondering whether to explain that he might be expecting too much. Before she could say anything, Rheinhard bowed his head and prayed. "Dear Jesus, You can do everything. I know that You can. You will send my mother back to me. . . ."

Majken had recorded the story in her diary and had concluded by writing:

> That was almost three years ago, and Rheinhard never lets an evening go past without getting on his knees and repeating that prayer. He will do it tonight. He has the same conviction that he had when he first prayed. He has never doubted, he is only waiting patiently.

Three years later, Rheinhard and a small party of adults stood on the platform of the rail station at Eckernförde.

Rheinhard was quiet, waiting soberly. In his hand was a small bouquet of wild flowers that he had picked in the woods early that morning.

The train pulled into the station and hissed to a stop. A middle-aged woman dressed in a shabby woolen coat stepped off. She looked around and then her arms flew out in joy as she ran toward her son.

Seven years in a Siberian labor camp had taken its toll, but there was no doubt. Rheinhard's mother had come home.

# 14

## BARBED WIRE
## AND WATCH DOGS

The fourth house had been dedicated, and twenty-two more children were being cared for. They joined two hundred twenty other boys and girls who were daily fed, clothed, encouraged, and helped both physically and spiritually.

Majken began to feel uncomfortable at the amount of influence that she seemed to wield. It was not because she did any more or even as much as many of the others. She came to the realization that it was due to the fact that she was closely associated with the raising of funds. People seemed to defer to people who controlled money. This had never been Majken's intent, nor would she allow it to continue.

In discussing her feelings with Pastor Schreiber and the Sisters, it was concluded that it was time to incorporate the home. The name would be *"Mission Kinderheim,"* with a United States organization to be known as Refugee Children, Inc.

It was agreed that the board of directors should be active participants in the everyday working of the home, and that no projects would be undertaken without unanimous approval. Four countries were initially represented on the board: Germany, Sweden, the United States, and Canada.

With this accomplished, Majken felt relieved. No longer would she have to shoulder all the responsibilities. She had always thought of herself as "wearing a dress with no pockets." Now she would be able to make sure it continued in that way.

Several major projects still had to be completed at the home. First, there was the need for a chapel. There was one small church in the community of Eckernförde, but now there were over two hundred and fifty people at the home. This was more than the local church could hold; consequently many of the children could not attend each Sunday. The Board agreed that the home needed its own church.

It was also obvious that the border situation was reaching critical proportions. People were escaping by the thousands. Soon the Soviet Union would intervene. The West German government was now making large sums of money available for refugee work, and the geographics of the problem had shifted.

It was time to reassess the work. Majken packed a small suitcase and took off for Berlin.

She made two trips to Berlin within the space of a year; the two ran together into one experience in the aftermath of August '61.

She wrapped her coat around her to keep out the freezing October wind. Her mind went back to the headlines that had jumped out of the newspaper the previous months and she tried to make sense of the injustice that was being imposed on the people of Germany.

| | |
|---|---|
| July 13, 1961 | Mass flight from East Germany. The number of refugees coming each day has doubled. |
| July 14, 1961 | The Berlin crisis . . . The situation has never been more serious. There will be not one person left in East Berlin if the |

exodus of four hundred to five hundred a day continues.

| | |
|---|---|
| July 18, 1961 | Four thousand came into West Berlin today during the daylight hours only. |
| July 20, 1961 | The stream of refugees has increased. Every day from seven hundred to one thousand people flee from the East. |
| August 5, 1961 | Complete despair in the zone. Ten thousand five hundred fled in five days' time. |

Then on August 13, 1961, Soviet authorities had sealed the border. The newspapers declared: "The Berlin Wall is established. Refugees drop all along the border as the Soviet Union moves in more troops. Many die in a last attempt. Refugee influx into Germany down 98 percent from one month ago."

With the hundreds of native Berliners Majken had been shocked beyond belief. Their city, their country was divided. Now before her stood the Berlin Wall, only a small section of a 900-mile Iron Curtain, strewn with five hundred watch towers, barbed wire, armed guards, and watch dogs. Flares shot into the sky if the barbed wire moved. The "Wall" stretched from the shores of the Baltic in the North to Czechoslovakia. She had seen parts of it—former railway stations, now desolate with the tracks ripped away. Homes with barbed wire fences going in one side and out the other. Wreaths and crosses—a gruesome testimony to the fact that not everyone became a refugee.

One sign declared it *"Der Totesstreifen durch Deutschland"*—"The death line through Germany."

Everywhere she turned the tragedy was reenacted. Only, the actors and actresses were real people, whose one desire was to be free. Majken watched as two women, both middle-aged, approached an opening in the Wall. One of the

117

women wore a nurse's uniform and pulled a little wagon holding a suitcase. They walked slowly to the barrier. Several guards moved to stop them. Majken heard the women speak. "Mother, mother, when will I see you again?" "I do not know, I do not know." The words were lost in their embrace.

The two parted. One took out papers and handed them to a guard. She pulled her wagon through the opening into East Germany. Another family separated.

Coming the other way was not so simple. At first the people jumped from the windows of the houses along the Wall. The windows were soon sealed with cement.

Majken turned to a German boy watching her. He was about twelve years old.

"Do they still try to get through there?" she asked, pointing.

"Oh, yes," replied the boy, "almost every day someone tries to get across, but," he added sadly, "not many of them make it."

Majken studied the elaborate traps that the Communists had built to prevent escape—the trenches dug to keep trucks from ramming the fences, the concrete and steel barriers to discourage even the most daring drivers. She looked at the watch towers and thought of other concentration camps that she had seen. Night came on and still Majken watched. Floodlights threw the watch towers into stark relief against the darkness. Sparks popped and sizzled as the barbed wire was charged with high voltage.

She recalled the words spoken by a U. S. president who stood at the same wall: *"Ich bin Berliner"*—"I am a Berliner." It was a statement made, not as a promise to tear the Wall down, but as an apology for allowing it to be built at all. Later, another world leader from Moscow would say, "I have read that the American president looked very discontentedly at the Wall. He doesn't like it. But I like it. I like it extraordinarily well."

Majken also remembered the words of Lenin: "He who has Berlin, has Germany; he who has Germany has Europe."

Back in her little hotel room, Majken thought about the nurse pulling her little wagon back to East Germany. *What is she doing now?* she asked herself.

Tears flowed as Majken remembered the verse that she had seen written above a wreath of wilted flowers: *"Betet ohne unterlass."* "Pray without ceasing."

As she began to pray, the words of Deuteronomy came to mind: "The LORD, he is it that doth go before thee, he will be with thee, he will not fail thee, neither forsake thee: fear not, neither be dismayed."*

Night turned into morning. Life attempted to go on as normal in Berlin. The morning newspaper told of a young man who was killed while trying to escape.

Then, as it does each day at noon, the Freedom Bell, given by the people of the United States, rang. Majken heard it and remembered the words inscribed on it: "That this world, under God, shall have a new birth of freedom."

She left her hotel and walked to the Wall one last time. She thought of the children at the home, and silently, humbly, stood before the Wall and prayed.

"God, I thank You that we could rescue at least a few. I pray that they are the ones that will, under God, give a new birth of freedom to this land. God, never let our love for You be divided as this nation is. Never let Satan build wire fences and a no man's land between those who love You. Let our home be a symbol of love, bringing people together, not tearing them apart."

---

*Deut. 31:8.

119

# 15

# A NEW KIND
# OF REFUGEE

The Wall cut the refugee flow to a trickle; the rising economy and efficiency of the West German government in finding homes and reuniting families quickly cleared the cellars and the bomb shelters. Majken was encouraged as she toured, once again, the refugee centers. "But," one social worker told Majken, "we have a new problem. It is not Communism but materialism. There are many broken homes and much divorce. There are many children with special medical needs who need a place where they can be given another opportunity. Would you consider making a home for such children?"

Majken was already planning in her mind a clinic, to be used as a dormitory for "special" children.

Depressed by what she had seen at the border but full of plans for the future of the home, Majken arrived back at Eckernförde. Her enthusiasm was short-lived. Little Franz was dying.

Somberly, Majken, Sister Ruth, and Herr Schreiber drove to the hospital. All three still were deeply attached to the boy, although he had been home with his mother for a year.

"I guess he will never be the minister that he wanted to be," said Majken, breaking the silence in the car.

"Some people don't have to become adults before they

become ministers," said Sister Ruth, who knew Franz better than anyone else.

In a few minutes they were gathered around Franz's bed.

*He doesn't look sick*, thought Majken. *He looks as radiant as ever. I wonder if it is a mistake.* But when he spoke, Majken could see how sick he really was. His voice was very weak.

"Pastor Schreiber," said Franz, "read to me from the Bible. Read to me about the city with the gates of pearls, where there will be no more needles stuck into my arms, and no more headaches."

Reverently they listened as Pastor Schreiber complied.

"Dear Jesus," whispered Franz, "will You take my hand when I come through the gate?"

With Franz's hand in hers, Sister Ruth began to sing an old German folk hymn.

Take my hands and lead Thou me,
     Until in the land of light, Thee I see.

Franz, his voice almost transparent, smiled and joined in.

If in the darkness of the night,
     I cannot see Your hand, my Father
I know that You will take me across the dark water,
     And lead me to the shore.
Then take my hands and lead Thou me,
     Until in the bright land of light
I shall see Thee . . . face to face.

Early the next morning, the Savior Franz had come to know so well at Eckernförde took his hand, and together they crossed to the other shore.

121

# 16

# THE PROVIDER

The children never tired of asking Majken about the people who made the homes possible. She never tired of sharing the various stories with them, always making certain they understood that this was God's work. People were merely the channel for its provision.

She told of a small church in a far-away place called Westbrook, Maine. It had started in 1952, with only forty people who decided they would sacrificially give all they could for missions. "When I arrived in October of 1954, there were 125 people, and they were a blessing to people all over the world. Let me show you what I mean," said Majken.

"What do you do when it gets cold and you go outside to play? What do you do with your hands?"

"We put on our mittens," several children called out.

"And where did you get the mittens?"

"From Jesus," they replied.

"That's right. But who did Jesus use to give you the mittens?"

There was silence.

"I'll tell you. At this church there is a lady eighty-five years old. She had no money to give, but you know what she did?"

"What?" they cried.

"She knitted 185 pairs of mittens for you."

Their eyes round with wonder, the children gasped and whispered to each other. "A hundred eight-five mittens! And she made them for *us*!"

"Not only that, you know how it was so cold last winter, that some of you had to have extra blankets? Well, they were made by a lady eighty-eight years old."

Then Majken went on to tell about the woman who came to Jesus. All she had to give was an alabaster box of perfume. Majken explained how important this was to this lady, because she had used all of her money to buy it. The children listened intently. "At this church, a lady came to me and said, 'Majken, here is my alabaster box to help the children.' "

"An alabaster box?" asked one of the youngsters. "I don't remember seeing an alabaster box here."

"Well," replied Majken, "her alabaster box was a beautiful diamond ring!"

"Who has it now?" asked another.

"You do." said Majken."

"We do?" chimed in several of the children.

"That's right," said Majken, "we sold it for money to buy you food."

The stories continued. As she told them and retold them, more and more the children saw that God was at work, caring for them.

One of the ongoing needs was for shoes. Often to Majken it seemed as if the children were racing to see if it was faster to grow out of their shoes or to wear them out.

Majken was in Örebro, Sweden, showing pictures of the work in Eckernförde. It was an ordinary meeting, with polite but unenthusiastic interest. While Majken was folding up her equipment, a tall, white-haired man came up to her, smiled, and introduced himself. Bluntly he asked, "Miss Broby, do you need some shoes?"

Majken was so startled all she could say was yes.

"Very well," said the man, "I have a shoe store," and he handed Majken his card. "Come to my shop at eight tomorrow morning."

Promptly at eight o'clock, Majken appeared at the store. She thought there must be a mistake. There was a sign on the door which said the store did not open until nine. She was about to leave when the door opened. The owner invited Majken in and asked, "How many pairs do you need?"

Majken tried to think how many she could ask for graciously.

"You said you have two hundred children in the home, is that right?" asked the owner.

"Yes," said Majken, "that is right."

The man smiled and then with a sweep of his hand said, "We have gathered two hundred pairs. What is left over I will sell to the public, but I want your children to have the best. I will ship them to you."

The day the shoes arrived, so did the bill. Written across the bottom in bold strokes were the words, *Paid: For the sake of Jesus Christ.*

# 17

## RENEWED VISION

Christmas 1961 was only a couple of days away as Majken sat in the comfortable living room of Pastor and Mildred Hess. Their Connecticut home had come to be a refuge and a place of special blessing for Majken in her many travels across America.

Now she sat drinking coffee, eating Mrs. Hess's special almond Christmas cookies and enjoying the fresh smell of the pine Christmas tree that stood joyfully decorated in the corner.

The Lord had sent some very special people to Eckernförde in the same way that He had sent Majken years earlier. One such person was Dr. John Green of the National Association of Christian Congregational Churches (NACCC). The children won the heart of Dr. Green and a relationship began that would grow over the years, opening up churches throughout America who belonged to NACCC.

But in spite of all that the Lord had done, Majken sensed that there was more—and He wanted her involved.

She had been so busy meeting day-by-day needs that there was not much time for a longer look. But a feeling of discontent kept surfacing during her time of prayer and Bible study. She had not felt this way since her days as an

X-ray technician in Sweden. She remembered how the headlines about anything happening in Germany had jumped out at her. The vision of hollow eyes and out-stretched arms had persisted even though she kept protest-ing, "Not Germany, Lord. Not after what they have done to Your people."

Lately, she had been drawn to anything that mentioned Muslims and Africa. However, she was too involved in the present work to give it much thought. She was working hard, but her health was good, and she looked forward to returning to Eckernförde after Christmas.

Twenty-four hours later, the fragrance of Christmas pine had been replaced by the familiar antiseptic smell of a hospital room. The stabbing pains in her chest had come quickly. She had gone to bed certain that she had only picked up a little cold, and that she would feel better in the morning.

A visit by Pastor Hess's doctor dispelled any such hope. She had been in the hospital only a few hours when the doctor came and told her that she had a pulmonary embolism caused by a blood clot in her leg. If it moved into her heart it could be fatal. She must remain in the hospital and lie perfectly still.

Christmas Eve in the hospital! Despite her best intentions to be patient, she became angry. *Why, Lord? I was looking forward to spending this night with those whom I love.*

The words came back, *You are, Majken.*

Self-pity turned to shame and then to joy as she went back to another Christmas in Germany. Memories flooded her mind. Pastor Schreiber had asked, "How can we make a *real* Christmas for the children here?" Food was short; pres-ents were impossible. But a few days before Christmas someone gave them a sack of oatmeal and dried milk and four dollars.

"We can buy a Christmas tree," said Pastor Schreiber to

126

the Sisters. "And maybe a few small presents for the children."

In their Bible study they studied the words of Jesus: "It is more blessed to give than to receive." Afterward, the Bible was closed, and Herr Schreiber asked the children, "How would you like to spend Christmas?"

In a short time all agreed. Eighteen miles from the home was a refugee camp for old people. "Let's make cookies with our oatmeal and go sing some Christmas songs for them."

The room came alive with excitement. "Let's use our pfennigs to buy candles," cried one youth. "Let's take the dried milk and give them milk and the cookies as a gift," volunteered another to enthusiastic applause.

Christmas Eve arrived. All day long the kitchen had smelled of baking, until the children could hardly endure the delicious aroma. That night the children boarded the bus giddy with anticipation. As their excitement grew they made Herr Schreiber stop along the way. Merrily they ran into the forest and gathered branches from evergreen trees.

At the camp the children burst off the bus and soon filled the room where the party was to be. The elderly people watched quite dazed as the children decorated the tables with candles and evergreens and proudly deposited a pitcher of milk and oatmeal cookies at each table.

Then, still solemn, the sixty refugees took their seats. The children's faces glowed in the candlelight as they sang the old familiar carols. Pastor Schreiber read the Christmas story and explained how God gave the gift of Christmas, His Son Jesus Christ. Tears flowed freely. The eyes of those forsaken people who had known such persecution began to light up as they joined in the singing. One old grandmother prayed, thanking God for sending the little children to remind them that Jesus also came as a child.

It was midnight before the children made their way

through the frosty night to the bus. Snow was gently falling, and the children continued to sing softly. It had been a memorable Christmas Eve for everyone. How good it was to have such a storehouse of memories from which to draw at times like this.

"But Lord, here I am with a blood clot in my leg," Majken said with a sigh. "How will I pay my hospital bills? Will I be able to continue to reach out to others?"

As her thoughts roved, newspaper headlines began to come into focus. She thought of the many articles she had clipped out of the papers about Muslims and North Africa.

"Lord," cried Majken, "I have never been to North Africa." She opened her Bible. "Lord, I need something now. Enlarge my vision."

She found herself in Psalms: "I shalt not die, but live, and declare the works of the LORD" (Ps. 118:17).

She set the Bible aside. She had God's promise.

"I will recover. I will live, and I will proclaim the works of God. And Lord, when you tell me to, I will go to North Africa."

# *18*

# A MOTHER'S LOVE

Majken spent the next six months in the United States, Sweden, and Germany. There were letters to read and answer—inquiries from interested people. It was more than enough to occupy her time.

She continued to search the papers for articles on Muslims and North Africa. She found that there were indeed many Muslims in North Africa, almost one million of them. She had discovered that Pastor Schreiber was also interested in North Africa and that he had made some inquiries about needs in Morocco.

She was in Eckernförde when she received the telegram from her brother in Sweden: "Can you come? Mother has had a heart attack."

She sat for a few moments, gathering her thoughts. No one else had been so close to her as her mother. Joy, sorrow, everything that came Majken's way, she shared with her mother, and every day, no matter where Majken was, she knew that her mother was praying for her.

For some years, Sigrid Broby had not been well. A well-meaning friend had said to Majken, "Don't you feel that you should care for your mother?" But Mrs. Broby would not hear of it.

"Majken, how could anyone even think such a thing?

God has called you to a great work. God will take care of both of us."

In a few hours the plane landed in Gothenburg. Majken rushed to her mother's bedside and held her mother's hand. Slowly, her mother opened her eyes, smiled at Majken, and spoke for the first time since her attack. "I have seen Jesus. I feel peaceful and at rest."

Slowly Mrs. Broby gained new strength, and Majken treasured every hour that she spent with her. But a difficult decision had to be made. Majken had promised to be in the United States for some crucial meetings. It wasn't necessary to tell Mrs. Broby the predicament; she had sensed it already.

"Majken, do you remember when you were a little girl, and we thought you were dying?"

"Yes, Mother, I remember."

"One day I knelt down and told God that if He would spare your life, I would never claim you for myself." She looked at her daughter lovingly and reached for her hand. "Majken, always remember: God's kingdom is first. You must go to America. Come back when you are through. I will pray for you. If it is God's will that we meet again here, we will. If the Lord takes me home, we will meet in heaven."

"Mother," said Majken, "never has my heart been so torn." But she had her answer.

She leaned over and kissed her mother. They were both in tears, but they were tears of peace and joy only tinged with sadness.

Majken set out for the United States at once, but every day she wrote her mother, telling of her experiences. She knew that her mother loved picture postcards, so she bought several each time she stopped and mailed them along the way.

From Chicago she crossed the plains to Montana and

North Dakota. She was in Minneapolis, heading back east-wards when she received the telephone call from her cousin. "Majken, I am sorry, but your mother has gone to be with the Lord." It was a long, lonely drive back to Illinois. There were many friends waiting at her cousins' home when she arrived, who had come to offer their condolences. Among them was an elderly man from Prairieview, Illinois, who drew her aside privately.

"Majken, I know your mother's spirit is with God, but He has put it on my heart that you should be home to see her one last time."

He reached out with trembling hands and handed Maj-ken an envelope. It contained the money for a roundtrip ticket to Sweden.

While waiting at the airport in New York, Majken tele-phoned her friend, Elma Cook, in Florida to tell her the news.

"Majken," said Elma, "I know that this may sound like a very strange request from me, but I feel that you are very close to me. You know I have never had any children of my own." She paused for a moment and then continued in a voice trembling with emotion, "Is it too much to ask you to call me Mom? There will never be another 'Mother' for you, but I can be a 'Mom.' I'd like to fill part of the gap. I will pray for you every day, and my prayers will follow you wherever you go."

*Before I asked, Lord, you have answered*, thought Majken. With deep gratitude she told Elma how God had just met one of her greatest needs. It had been a point of anguish to Majken, since hearing of her mother's death, that no one would faithfully support her with prayer.

When Majken arrived in Sweden she went directly to the funeral home. She thought she had never seen her mother look so beautiful. With a gentle sigh she sat before her and began to talk.

"Mother, this is the first time that you won't be able to answer me. But I have so many good things to tell you, I know that you will hear."

She told her how much she had meant to her. She told her how much her prayers had influenced her to be a servant of the Lord. And she told her how dangerous it must be to live in this world without a praying mother.

"Mother, it was you that led me to Jesus, not just by what you said, but by how you lived. No matter where I traveled, I felt secure, because I knew that wherever in this world the Lord might take me, you were praying for me."

Majken poured out her heart until at last she felt at peace. She had one more thing to say. "Mother, the Lord has provided me someone new to care for me as you did, but your life will continue to be a part of me."

# 19

# "ABSOLUTELY IMPOSSIBLE!"

Back in her little room in Eckernförde, Majken found herself spending more and more time studying about North Africa. She had an almost insatiable curiosity, especially about the country of Morocco. She was fascinated by its rich history, which started in the twelfth century before Christ, and by the influence that Islam had had upon the country since the Muslim conquest in 670 A.D.

Studies of the poor living conditions—aggravated by a 2.5 percent annual increase in the population—revealed that many of the people outside of the big cities had difficulty in simply staying alive. Though there were health facilities in the large cities of Tangier, Rabat, and Marrakesh, it was quite a different story in the outlying regions. Majken could only imagine what the small villages were like, and how much help they needed. Certainly there were plenty who were naked, hungry, and without a roof over their heads.

Majken was not alone in her burden. Herr Schreiber had continued his interest in Morocco. He pored over maps of the region and was especially interested in the small groups of nomadic peoples who moved from oasis to oasis. Often he imagined what it would be like to go into the desert and build a village equipped with water. He constructed models of his ideas and used them as prayer targets, in the same way that blueprints had been used in planning, praying, and then building the homes at Eckernförde.

After much prayer and consultation, it was decided that Majken, Herr Schreiber, and two Sisters would take the old Volkswagen bus to make a survey trip of Morocco. They would travel through Germany and Switzerland to Spain, then ferry across the Straits of Gibraltar to Tangier.

By the time the six-day journey was over, they had agreed to investigate two avenues of service. First, they would seek out young boys and girls who needed a home and an education. Then they would make arrangements to bring them to Eckernförde for as long as necessary. Second, they would attempt to make contacts with government officials who could recommend where they might build a model village, with adequate housing, irrigation, and a clinic. They realized that this was a Muslim nation, and that their initial witness had to be on more subtle terms than they were accustomed to using.

In their initial contacts in Tangier they were informed that both of their desires were "absolutely impossible." No Moroccan, no matter how destitute, would allow his children to be taken from a Muslim home and taught in the house of an infidel. Furthermore, the people of the desert were nomadic and suspicious of outsiders. They had been poor and lived primitively for centuries, and they could never be changed.

Local missionaries had even less encouragement to offer.

Each day Herr Schreiber and his companions prayed anew, "Father, you brought us here; now continue to lead us." They had nearly exhausted their contacts when they were informed of an Anglican missionary named Wilson— "or something like that"—who worked in the desert. He lived near the foot of the Atlas Mountains, at least two hundred miles away, an almost impossible journey.

With little encouragement from man but much assurance

134

from God, the four climbed into their VW and headed for the little-known city of Denmar. Paved roads turned to packed sand. The sides of the road were marked sporadically with a few stones.

The sun began to set, an enormous crimson ball against the vast colorlessness of the desert. The blue-shadowed mountains served as their only compass. It was a chain 484 miles long that stretched the full length of the country, an effective barrier separating the "people" from the "tribes." Nearly all the peaks exceeded sixty-five hundred feet, with some over two miles high.

They made camp at nightfall, and with the first light of day, they were driving again, the trip endless in the vast mirage of the desert.

They prayed, they drove, and they perspired. The sun was just beginning to set on the second day when they spotted a cluster of square, mud-colored buildings. They had passed several groups of people on the way, but none of them spoke German, English, Swedish, or French. Nevertheless the nomads, staring blatantly at the curious band, had pointed towards the mountains when Herr Schreiber asked, "Denmar?"

They stopped on the outskirts of what appeared to be a city of maybe two or three hundred inhabitants. The VW quickly drew a curious crowd of onlookers. The children were dressed only in dirty rags. Herr Schreiber asked in German if they knew of a man named Wilson. "Is this Denmar? Do you speak English?" All of the questions were met with smiles, laughs, nods, but no verbal reply. Finally, one of the Sisters asked in French, "Is this Denmar?" An older person stepped forward and replied in kind. "Yes, this is Denmar." A broken exchange of gestures and extremely bad French brought them to the door of a delapidated hut, the home of the "God man."

The Reverend Wilson, a tall, slender man with the

countenance of an ascetic, welcomed them with immediate empathy. Quickly he prepared a small table of refreshments, and soon was speaking freely of his work. He had established a small clinic and a school where people were taught to read and write. Their main text was the Bible.

"However," he told them, "I am looking for the opportunity to help the children on a more permanent basis."

Pastor Schreiber and Majken explained to Wilson how they had been led to Morocco. "We would like to find some children that we could take to Eckernförde for an education," began Majken, when Rev. Wilson put his head in his hands, whispered a short prayer, and then clasped their hands with joy.

"The Lord has sent you to the right place. One of my most faithful Christian workers died only a short while ago. He was only thirty years old, but he contracted tuberculosis and by the time we got medical help, it was too late. His wife is still a strong Muslim. I sat beside this brother as he died. His last words were 'Dear Lord Jesus, please send someone who will take my children and raise them in a Christian home.'

"Since he died the children have had a very difficult time. They wake up in the morning and ask for food, but there is none. They go to bed as hungry as when they awake. The girls have been sent to a relative, but there is no room for the three boys. I have been bringing them to my home for one meal a day."

The next day, they visited the mother and she readily agreed to release the three boys for schooling. Wilson was certain that with her consent the officials would grant them permission.

The group left Denmar and went to the capital city of Rabat, where Wilson had given them the name of another woman who might want to send her children to Eckernförde. Again the mother agreed. Almost as an afterthought she was asked, "Do you have any government contacts? We would like to investigate other opportunities while we are here."

"Yes," she replied unexpectedly. "My son-in-law works with the government. I am sure he would be happy to introduce you to the proper authorities." The man proved to be very interested in Herr Schreiber's sketches for wells and irrigation facilities.

"You have seen our buildings," said the son-in-law. "They crumble when there is too much sun; they collapse when there is too much rain. Many of our people live in ruins. Come, I would like my superior to talk to you."

After interviews with two higher officials, Herr Schreiber and the Sisters were ushered into the office of the Secretary of State, who gave them the name of the governor of southern Morocco. "I believe he is visiting in the oasis near Sagura."

Later the next day the VW pulled into the city of Sagura, and the visitors found themselves greeted by two army jeeps full of soldiers. One of the men began a friendly conversation in French.

Majken finally asked him if he knew where the governor might be.

"You are fortunate," said the man. "He comes here but once a year to begin his annual inspection of the South. He is here now and will be leaving early tomorrow morning."

"We would like to see him," said Majken. "Can you help us?"

"*Madame,* I am his personal attendant," said the man with obvious pride. "I will personally introduce you."

Soon they found themselves in the only hotel in the city, seated on the floor of a large room gaily decorated with rugs. A troupe of veiled dancing girls was performing, but the governor was oblivious to the entertainment. He was intently speaking to Herr Schreiber on his right and Majken on the left.

The evening became late and finally the governor rose.

"We leave at five in the morning. I invite you to accompany me for an inspection tour as my personal guests."

Traveling with the governor was like traveling with a king. As they arrived at each oasis they were met by the entire village. The people bowed deeply, more than ready with music, dancing, and food. Late in the day, they reached the oasis of BouRbia. It was like the other villages—clay buildings in disrepair, people living from day to day.

As they stood in a palm grove, four tired travelers wondering if they were not just tourists who happened to get a ride with the governor, Majken heard herself pray, "Lord, where do you want us to start?"

The words were interrupted by the governor.

"This is a very needy oasis. Why don't you begin your work here? I will tell the people you are coming back, and you will be welcome."

One week later, the four from Eckernförde, with seven Moroccan children, were on the ferry crossing the Straits of Gibraltar, homeward-bound. It was a route they would travel many times in the future, realizing each time that what is "impossible" with man, has already been established by the Lord.

# 20

# A PLACE
# TO WORSHIP

The children from Morocco—six boys and a girl—adjusted quickly to Eckernförde. Majken wished that she were so content. The trip to Morocco had kept her mind occupied, but now the daily routine of opening mail, writing letters, and working with the children, allowed the ache of her losses to seep through. Two people who had been so much a part of her life, her mother and Franz, were gone. Majken had given her heart to many children during the past year, but when they left to live with their families, there was always a void. Majken was an "auntie" to many, but she wanted to be a mother.

She began to investigate, and soon word came from France that a little girl, barely a year old, was available for adoption. "Lord, is it possible that she could be mine?" prayed Majken. The pressure was intense; the level of doubt among her friends was high.

"Majken, how will you ever be able to drag a child around to all of your meetings?"

"Majken, it is one thing to be an auntie, but quite another to be a mother."

Initially the judge involved in the case advised, "A forty-six-year-old single missionary, who travels all over the world, may not make a very good mother. Perhaps you should not consider it."

Sister Ella, a mother to many girls at the home, was a ray of hope. "Motherhood is not in how much you travel, but in how much you love."

"Lord, is it possible that this little girl could be mine?" asked Majken again and again.

After two months of Majken's persistence and prayers, the judge in France said it was "highly irregular" but signed the papers. Majken had a daughter, Christine.

She accompanied her mother wherever she traveled, no matter how far. During their trips to America, she sat in the front row and read a hymnal upside down or crawled under the pulpit (where no one would see her) and sat at her mother's feet during the service.

On one such trip they came to Los Angeles, California. Together they visited a man with whom Majken had been corresponding. Robert Roy was a civil engineer for the U.S. Army, who gave much of his time and substance to mission work around the world. He heard about Majken's work and wanted to become involved.

When they visited his home, he admitted that he could offer no contacts, only a deep conviction that he should talk to Majken and see if somehow he could be of help.

She told him about Eckernförde—their desire for a clinic-dormitory for special boys and girls and a chapel which had not yet been fulfilled.

Roy explained in turn how he had been seeking God's guidance in what he might do for Majken. "Last night I felt very strongly about calling the people at a radio program here in Los Angeles. Have you ever heard the program *Haven of Rest*?" he inquired.

Majken had not.

"Many times the quiet teaching of God's Word and the music has been a great comfort to me," he related. "I think they would understand your work."

He had no idea who to contact or even what to say when

he telephoned. "I would like to talk to someone about a mission project," he said simply.

He ended up speaking with Val Hellikson, and he briefly explained about Majken's work. "I know that you must receive many calls like this," Roy said, half apologetically, "but I think you would like to talk to Miss Broby."

"Tell me," Mr. Hellikson inquired, "does this woman of whom you are speaking, does she have need of a church or a chapel?"

Roy was taken aback. "Why, yes, yes, she does. How did you know?"

"Well," continued Mr. Hellikson, "at our prayer meeting this morning each of us was under a strong impression that we should help build a chapel or church somewhere in the world. We did not know where or when. I think you should bring Miss Broby over to see us."

When Majken left Los Angeles the next day her heart was overflowing with joy. The Haven of Rest had promised to raise the twenty-five thousand dollars to build the chapel at Eckernförde.

It was the beginning of a long relationship that through the years would involve many projects on two different continents, in addition to a monthly pledge for the continuing operation at Eckernförde.

# 21

# TO DREAM THE
# IMPOSSIBLE DREAM

Majken, Sisters Lydia and Ella, Christine, and three Moroccan boys manuevered into the only space left inside the station wagon. The rear end nearly touched the ground as they attempted to settle in along with clothes, medical supplies, and a couple of electrical generators. Water pipes were tied securely on top of the car.

Despite looks of apprehension, mingled with silent prayers from the Sisters and a few giggles from the children, Majken carefully guided the car down the drive of the home. Destination: Morocco, North Africa.

After traveling less than an hour, Majken looked in the rearview mirror to see the flashing red lights of a police car signaling her to pull over.

"Lady," said the policeman, "you are driving in a dangerous manner."

"But officer," protested Majken, "I am driving slowly and I have not broken the law."

"Your car is almost dragging the pavement. Don't you realize that you could scrape your gas tank on the pavement and set your vehicle on fire?"

Majken pleaded her case. The policeman looked first incredulous, then sympathetic and discomfited as Majken explained that she was on her way to the Sahara Desert. The pump was needed for a well, the pipe to transfer the water, the medical supplies for the sick, and the three children were being returned to their parents for a vacation.

"Well, lady, I won't give you a ticket, but you won't get many more miles before another policeman stops you and has you unload some of this stuff."

"Lord, blind the eyes of the policemen," Majken prayed as she continued through Germany and into Switzerland. The customs officer looked at her, the car and its occupants and supplies and shrugged his shoulders, waving them on.

It was 1965, and Majken was finally realizing the second chapter of her vision of long ago. The work at Eckernförde was firmly established—the stakes were laid out now for the new chapel—and miraculously the money had come in for the new venture: Morocco. With a smile she realized that her many trips across the United States had been excellent training for this journey. The company of Sister Lydia, Sister Ella, and little Christine made the drive seem almost easy.

Five days later they reached the ferry, now a familiar sight to Majken. The cool breeze from the Mediterranean refreshed everyone. The customs officers checked Majken's papers, scanning her car and its cargo, then they glanced at each other, frowned, and asked about the three Moroccan boys. "We are bringing them home for vacation," said Majken. "Their parents live in Rabat."

Thus began the last lap of their journey, a twelve hour drive to the south of Morocco.

The children were very excited as they drew closer to home, but all Majken could think of was the Atlas Mountains. She had crossed them once before, but in the governor's Jeep. How would her station wagon make it?

After delivering the children to their mother, there was space to stash extra liters of gasoline and water. They headed for the oasis of BouRbia. Ahead lay unmarked roads, a treacherous mountain range, and miles and miles of hot, blazing desert.

The station wagon moved steadily over the narrow road and up and over Mount Atlas. Majken and her passengers laughed all the way down the other side. The great barrier to the Sahara had been conquered by three women and a child. But as the cool mountain air turned to the heat of the desert they began to wonder if their rejoicing had been premature.

With delight little Christine drew their attention to the purple flowers that dotted the scenery. Later in the afternoon they came to a river, a welcome relief from the hot car. With glee the four waded into the water, washing and splashing like children. There was, however, one problem: no bridge for the car. Sister Ella bravely crossed the mild current, testing the river bed with her bare feet. It proved solid enough, with many large smooth stones. She climbed up the sand on the other side and cheered them on, as the car cautiously entered the stream. Water began to seep inside the car, and the motor sputtered but never stalled. To the sound of the roaring engine and spinning wheels, Sister Lydia added a shout of joy.

"Who needs bridges!" she shouted as they opened the doors to let the water out.

Finally, the night, which comes so quickly in the desert, engulfed them. The roads were dangerous enough in the daytime; to drive them at night would invite disaster. With this in mind they quickly cooked supper over a small butane burner and crawled back into the car to sleep.

Early the next morning, before the sun came over the horizon, they began what they hoped would be the last day of their journey.

After several hours they came to another river. Again they gratefully washed and tested the bottom for stones. Lydia, now the expert in river crossings, waded ahead.

Several times she sank knee-deep in mud. There were very few rocks on the bottom. However, this river was only about half as wide as the last one. The method of crossing was obvious: back up, gun the motor, and speed through.

Majken shifted the car into reverse. Lydia waited on the other side. This time she could not find it in herself to shout words of encouragement but waited tensely. Majken floored the accelerator and headed for the river. Lydia shouted as the car settled onto the sand on the other side. "Why, it was just like crossing the Red Sea," said Lydia as she opened the door. "The water just parted and you came through."

Early in the afternoon Sister Lydia was certain that she spied some trees ahead. Majken stopped the car and got out to investigate. They all agreed, including Christine who had the best eyes of all: It must be BouRbia. Majken refrained from telling them that people often saw mirages in the desert, but she did warn them that measuring distance in the desert was, at best, a fragile art. The sun's rays distorted one's perception, and the oasis might be as far as three or four hours away. Although they could see for miles in one direction, they should not assume that they could be seen from another vantage point equally far away. The road ahead was still dangerous, and the trip was not yet over.

As though to emphasize her point, Majken soon felt the car sinking into the soft sand. She gunned the engine and lurched forward. She traveled about thirty feet when again the wheels began to spin. She stepped on the gas, but this time instead of lurching forward, the wheels spun deeply into the sand.

They all got out and surveyed the back end of the car, buried in the sand.

Despite the intense heat the three women immediately began removing the wire mats tied to the top of the car. They had been ordered by Herr Schreiber for just such a time as this. Majken had never used them before, but Schreiber's directions had been explicit.

She tried to remember what she had been taught. First, a wooden board was put under the back bumper. A car jack was then placed on the board. When it became obvious that the jack would not fit under the bumper, she pulled out a shovel and dug a hole, placing the board into the hole and then maneuvering the jack into place. They took turns jacking up the back of the automobile. They took the mats, which were about eight feet long and eighteen inches wide, and placed one under each wheel. Carefully they lowered the car, started the engine and drove the length of the wire mats. Too late, she realized she was traveling too fast: She overshot her distance, and again the rear of the car was buried.

Four times they repeated the process. In three and a half hours, they had gone thirty-two feet.

The sun beat down relentlessly, the heat piercing their bodies. Majken knew they had to reach the oasis by nightfall. They had eaten all of their food. To survive on the desert another day, they each needed two gallons of water. They had a little less than three gallons of water left.

The car traveled a short distance and then sunk into the sand. This time it drove the mats deep into the sand under the car. As they surveyed the scene, they felt like they had lost the battle.

They agreed that the first priority was to lighten the car. As sweat mingled with their tears, they removed the water pump and pipe from the top of the car. The equipment inside the car was taken out and stacked alongside the road.

Their faces burned by the hot sand, their hands blistered by jacking the car up, the three stopped to rest, exhausted. Together they prayed and asked God for help and renewed physical strength. One more time they jacked the rear of the car. But they could not budge the wire mats.

146

Again they prayed. Suddenly, Majken remembered the rubber mats covering the floor of the car. Why wouldn't they work?

With renewed energy, they removed the mats and placed them between the tires and the wire.

Another prayer—this time for mercy.

Majken gently revved the motor and slipped the gearshift into drive. The wheels spun a few times, then they caught hold and the car lurched forward and kept going. Majken did not slow down until she knew that she was on hard sand.

Painfully, they dragged the water pump and the pipes and retied them on top of the car, securing them with the wire mats.

An hour later, to the complete amazement of the people of BouRbia, three bedraggled ladies and a very tired child emerged from a dirty, sand-encrusted station wagon and asked for a place where they might rest.

The next morning they took off for their target: the new oasis. The innkeeper understood their sign language and pointed them in what they hoped would be the right direction.

Though BouRbia had a population of only a hundred and five, they felt as though they were leaving civilization behind. One mile beyond BouRbia they noticed tire tracks in the sand, which led them to several tents among some ruins.

Pastor Schreiber, who had preceded them by a month, welcomed them to their new oasis. Looking around, Majken could see nothing but three tents and several buildings in a state of disrepair.

Pastor Schreiber was eager to discuss their work.

It was obvious that no help had been given to the desert people in the past. The people had nothing.

Pastor Schreiber explained why they could not begin

their work in BouRbia. It would be taking the gospel to the elite instead of helping those who needed it most. He explained that they had moved one mile from BouRbia so that when they dug their well, they would not be accused of tapping the underground springs that fed BouRbia.

Pastor Schreiber drew out the plans he had sketched: five cottages and one clinic. But first, they must concentrate on drilling a well. He had driven a VW jeep and had brought in the equipment necessary for that part of the project.

"Look around us," said Pastor Schreiber, "there is no reason why we cannot help these people make the desert bloom."

Together they read John 15:16, "Ye have not chosen me, but I have chosen you and ordained you, that ye should go and bring forth fruit, and that your fruit should remain: that whatsoever you shall ask of the Father in my name, he may give it you."

Majken had visions of what could be done for the people in the Sahara. She had dreamed her dreams and had drawn up plans with Herr Schreiber, but now she realized, as never before, that in the end a vision must find fruition through the sweat of the brow. To build an oasis where there were no trees, no water, and only a few broken-down houses and a couple of tents was going to take not just faith, but hard work.

With little Christine by her side, Pastor Schreiber showed Majken to her new home. It was one of the houses that had collapsed. They took a few steps down into what appeared to be a tomb. Though it was mid-morning, it was dim inside. There were no windows.

"This will be the safest place for you," said Pastor Schreiber. "We have considerable company at night—rats, mice, and snakes—but this way, their entrance is limited to one door."

Majken surveyed her temporary home with more than a little apprehension, but Christine found it exciting.

The afternoon was taken up with resting from their travels. In the evening, the Sisters and Herr Schreiber joined Majken and Christine for the first meal in their new dwelling. Pastor Schreiber placed several large traps outside their front door as he bade them good night, and they crawled into their sleeping bags. Rather nervously Majken reached over and zipped Christine's up as high as possible.

Majken slept lightly and was awakened several times during the night by the snapping of one of the traps.

When morning light began to filter in through the doorway, Majken peered cautiously to ascertain that there were no "guests" in the way and carefully crawled out of her sleeping bag. She shook her shoes to make sure no spider or scorpion had laid claim to a new homestead and, bending down, headed for the door.

She stopped, stunned by what lay before her, and then before Christine could awaken, quickly removed the eight traps across the entranceway. Each held a rat the size of a cat. She later found out that you caught as many rats as you set traps for.

The car had been unpacked and was ready for another trip. If a clinic was to be built, the outsiders would have to win the confidence of the people. The first step was to visit with people of other oases. Medical treatment would come later.

Majken had seen advertisements of oases in magazines. Somehow the impression was given that they were beautiful areas, adorned with tall palms, loaded with exotic fruits, women dressed in bright apparel, children playing in the streets, and camels standing by to carry some sheik off to another adventure. What she discovered proved to be a decided contrast.

Each of the oases was identical. The houses were in various conditions of disrepair, some no more than piles of rubble. There were a few sickly-looking olive trees.

Sister Ella, Sister Lydia, and of course, Christine, joined

her for her first expedition. When they arrived at the oasis, the women came running to greet them. Several women motioned them inside a one-room home with floors and walls made of dirt. There was no furniture. Several mats lay on the floor.

In one corner an older woman wrapped in a black chador was grinding grain between two stones. Two young women were breast-feeding naked children, and in another corner stood a goat, mouth open, panting from the heat. Stroking the goat was a solemn child perhaps eight or nine years old. She wore a burlap sack with one hole cut for her head and two slits on either side for her arms. Written across the front were the words, "This grain is a gift from the people of the United States of America."

*We too come with a gift*, thought Majken, as she accepted a small glass of what appeared to be hot peppermint tea. *May we give them more than food and clothing, Lord*, she prayed silently. *May we show them the Bread of Life, Jesus.*

Communication between Majken and the women—so far removed in their culture and their thinking—was difficult until they found a common denominator—the children. Majken, in a gesture of friendship, motioned to one of the children present to come closer. As he approached, Majken saw that his eyes were filled with pus.

Horrified, Majken checked his eyes and then tried to tell the mother, "Come to our place, and I will put medicine in his eyes." Majken wasn't sure she was understood, but then another woman brought her child to Majken. Her eyes were also filled with pus. Again Majken repeated the invitation.

The afternoon passed quickly. There was much to be learned. On the way back they no longer needed to wonder where their ministry would be. The need for the clinic and water was urgent. *But*, thought Majken, *while Pastor Schreiber and his helpers dig the well and build the clinic I must go to the people and do what I can.*

The work in the Sahara had officially started, and there was no turning back.

The morning after her first venture out into the oases, Majken was awakened early and informed that she had company. In less than forty-eight hours after her arrival the clinic was a reality. The women whom they had visited had understood Majken's sign language. The word had spread quickly, and there was a host of women outside, sitting patiently with their children, waiting for treatment.

Majken got out her black medical bag and went to work. First she cared for the children, but the adults had come as well, men and women.

One man came with an infection in his leg, which, like the children's eyes, needed little more than to be washed out. His arm had been cut off below the elbow. Majken pointed to the arm, asking, "What happened?"

The man took a little stone and moved it along the ground making a hissing sound, and then quickly hit his elbow with the stone. Majken got the message. He had been bitten by a snake, and his people had cut off his arm. The villagers had never heard of anesthetic. *There is little wonder*, she thought to herself, *that they do not flinch when I pour antiseptic on their open wounds. They have endured so much worse pain, that this is nothing.*

The ailments were as numerous as the people. Day by day, Majken stood out in the open, bending over women, men, and children washing wounds, applying antiseptic, and quietly praying that God would heal. Little by little she began to run out of medicine, but she determined to stay until her supplies were exhausted.

Early one morning, a woman appeared at Majken's doorway, motioning for her to follow. It was an hour's drive to the woman's oasis, during which she explained through signs that a child had been bitten. Majken assumed it was a snake bite.

When they arrived at the dilapidated house, Majken discovered her patient was a boy about five years old. His left arm was badly mangled. His father explained, again in crude sign language, that a wild dog had attacked the child.

For almost an hour, Majken worked to clean the wound. The boy never made a murmur. "If the dog does not have rabies," she told the woman, knowing helplessly that she did not understand, "the boy will live. If the dog has rabies, then he will die."

Snake bites, scorpions, TB, malnutrition, wild dogs—Majken continued to treat anyone who came for help.

Meanwhile, the men from BouRbia arrived each morning to help Pastor Schreiber dig the well. Those not involved in the digging picked up stones to clear the land. Along with the five cottages, Pastor Schreiber envisioned a vegetable plot and olive groves with the help of irrigation.

Finally, Majken ran out of supplies. It was time to take the children back to Eckernförde, and Sister Ella and Sister Lydia needed also to return. Majken would return to the oasis with medicine and medical equipment that was so desperately needed.

As they waved good-bye, Majken stepped on the gas pedal. She was in a hurry not just to get to Eckernförde, but to return to "her" oasis. And little Christine agreed.

# 22

# MISADVENTURE IN THE SAHARA

It was a beautiful Sunday morning in Eckernförde. Majken was surrounded by nearly three hundred people, but her thoughts were hers alone. How long she had prayed for this moment! She remembered that morning in Los Angeles when Mr. Roy had called the radio people at Haven of Rest.

And now she was participating in the long anticipated dedication of the chapel at the home. The singing rolled up into the high ceiling and back again, "Great God we praise. . . ."

The children's choir sang, "I have decided to follow Jesus, I have decided to follow Jesus. . . ." Majken looked at their sweet, cherubic faces—these precious children gathered from throughout Europe and Morocco.

Her gaze turned to the simple, life-sized cross at the front of the church, placed to be the first thing seen upon entering. It was given as a memorial to Rev. Raymond Hess, the pastor from Connecticut who had carried a cross for Majken and for the children so many times, and who was now with the Lord. Majken thought of the lines that Pastor Hess had written shortly before his sudden death:

> I do not ask an easy place;
> I ask no gift of wealth.

153

I do not crave my dreams fulfilled,
  nor do I ask for health.
I only ask my Savior's smile
  to be my better part.
I only ask His cross to be
  laid deep within my heart.

Standing a short distance from Majken was Gerda, one of the first girls who had lived at the home. She wore the uniform of a student nurse. She had brought her first paycheck from the hospital and given it to the home just before the dedication.

On the other side of Majken, a few rows down, stood Christine, holding tightly onto Sister Ella's arm. Dear Sister Ella, who gave Majken encouragement when all others said she could never raise a daughter; Sister Ella who loved her children into eternal life. Gratitude welled up inside Majken for servants like this.

Quietly the concluding words were spoken, the third verse of the ninth chapter of First Kings. "And the LORD said unto him, I have heard thy prayer and thy supplication, that thou hast made before me: I have hallowed this house, which thou hast built, to put my name there forever; and mine heart shall be there perpetually." Then, back to work.

Between catching up on her correspondence and gathering and packing medical supplies, Majken managed time to review the work at Eckernförde with the Sisters. Since the Berlin Wall had been erected, most of the publicity was saved for those few brave souls who made one last heroic attempt to run the gauntlet of electric fences, watch dogs, and no man's land. Few succeeded, and as the days passed, fewer seemed to try. The Wall was now accepted as part of the tragic landscape of Europe.

Money was coming in daily for the final of the six buildings that were planned at Eckernförde—the clinic-dormitory. Social workers had already requested that seventeen deaf-mute children from Berlin be placed in the facility to receive special training.

With her mind at rest about the home, Majken turned her full attention to another trip to the Sahara. The last of the medical supplies arrived and Majken began to pack her station wagon. Once again she packed until the rear of the car was almost touching the ground. With fond farewells to Sister Ella, Sister Ruth, and the children, Majken and Christine were on the road again.

The trip was not nearly so tiring as the first one, mostly because the land was familiar and Christine was her only distraction. She was a good traveler, and rarely complained. For the most part she lay her head on her mother's lap and slept or talked, while Majken drove. The miles and hours passed much quicker than they expected.

By the time they drove off the ferry at Tangier they both were surprised at how rested they felt. It was early morning, so they loaded the car with the gasoline and water needed for desert travel.

They spent the night at the foot of the Atlas Mountains, sleeping in the car. Early the next morning they began the four-hour climb. Majken felt like the mountain range was an old friend who would not cause them to suffer the same hardships others experienced, as evidenced by the grim ruins of cars and Jeeps strewn along the roadside and at the bottom of the ridges.

On the other side of the mountain, Majken set her compass for BouRbia. The car was hugging the sand all the way, and every once in a while the bottom would scrape the various rocks protruding out of the sand. The two rivers on the route were high, but Majken barely slackened her pace as she crossed them.

About two hours from their oasis Christine sat upright in

her seat. "Mommy, I smell gasoline," she said, wrinkling her nose.

Majken sniffed. The desert sometimes put out some strange odors, but never gasoline. Christine was right. Majken could smell it. She brought the car to a stop and stepped out into the blazing sun. With apprehension she walked to the rear of the car.

Christine spotted it first. Just under the right side a small gush of gasoline was shooting out of the tank. A stone had punctured it.

"Oh, Lord, what will we do?" prayed Majken. She had no idea how to stop the flow. They had used up all the reserve gas.

"Let's hurry, Mommy, and drive real fast so we won't run out of gas," urged Christine sprightly.

Majken hadn't any better ideas, so they jumped in the car and drove off. Speed in the desert is not what it is in other parts of the world. Five miles per hour is careful driving and fifteen is suicidal. Majken hovered between the two as she headed for BouRbia. She knew that when the car bottom scraped it was sending off sparks, and she also knew that she was leaving a trail of gasoline in the hot sun.

Fervently she prayed, doggedly maneuvering the car around the largest stones. She did not take time to check her compass but prayed that she was heading in the right direction.

"Look, Mommy, the needle is going down. Better hurry, Mommy," urged Christine, aware that there was danger.

The gas gauge was in the red zone. *How many miles left?* Majken asked herself.

Christine answered her question with a shout of glee. Dead ahead, glimmering in the sun was BouRbia. A few minutes later, Majken pulled in front of what in BouRbia was called a garage. She got out and looked at the tank. The flow of gasoline had stopped; the tank was empty.

# 23

## TURNING A DESERT INTO AN OASIS

With her return Majken was struck by the visible improvement in the oasis. The walls for two of the homes were rising. Thousands of the stones that once dotted the landscape had been gathered, and walls were being constructed marking off areas that would become olive groves.

The search for water continued, but the sand that was brought to the surface was still dry. Herr Schreiber had rigged a well using forty-gallon oil drums, a winch, and a chain attached to the frame. Water was still hauled from sixty miles away in barrels attached to the backs of camels and donkeys.

But miraculously, water had been found of a different kind. Hamid, the man who worked beside Pastor Schreiber, discovered the Living Water, and the two men met often—secretly—to drink from the fountain of life that never runs dry. It was a sensitive issue in this Muslim country, and not one that could be publicized.

A tent home had been made for Majken and Christine. They soon settled into a daily routine. Everyone was up at five A.M. and breakfasted on oatmeal and dried milk, or goat's milk if it was available. Majken then set out for the surrounding oases to visit the sick. The clinic that they were building would be of no use if they did not win the confidence of the people. Time and time again, Majken would enter an oasis unannounced to find people dying from some simple infection. They had never had medical help before, so they did not know it existed. Many stayed in their little huts to die rather than leaving their homes. Majken would have to bring the clinic to them.

On one especially hot day, Majken found herself cross-legged on the dirt floor of a little home four miles from her oasis. She was beginning to learn the local law of hospitality. No matter how poor they might be, their culture dictated that they be hospitable. Initially, Majken and Pastor Schreiber naively had hoped this was an acceptance of Christianity, but usually it wasn't.

The hostess was preparing peppermint tea while another woman began to mix food in a large wooden bowl. Even though she was not hungry and had not yet acquired a taste for Moroccan foods, she knew that in order to win these people's confidence she must come to them on their cultural level, and not hers.

Majken could see that for dinner they would have *koosh*, a white mush similar to cream of wheat. After grinding the grain, several women would knead it together with lard and some oil. It would then be placed over a fire and cooked for as long as two hours.

Majken still could not speak the language, so she sat by helpless, unable to protest, as they killed their only chicken. The hours passed.

Finally the *koosh* was ready. It was mixed with fresh goat's milk in a tin mug and passed from person to person. Majken stifled her nausea as she watched the mug lifted to lips covered with sores and handled by hands that had just rubbed an eye full of pus. To maintain her composure she concentrated on making mental notes as to the classes she would teach in the clinic on basic hygiene.

Her dismay grew as each person was given a spoon and a

clay pot was set in the midst of them. The others moved in close and motioned Majken to take some of the food. She dipped her spoon into the food first, and all the rest followed. It was a combination of chicken gruel and many other things that Majken tried not to think about. Together they sat and visited, even though they did not understand each other's language, until the bowl was empty.

Another woman brought a small bowl with water in it, a precious commodity that had been hauled many miles. Each person dipped their hands in the water and then wiped them on a towel passed from person to person. Majken wondered how many times the cloth had been used and for what purpose. Another note to add to her health class.

The lady of the house brought Majken a small necklace made from brightly dyed seeds and placed it around Majken's neck. Majken reached up and affectionately rubbed it, nodding and thanking her hostess for such a beautiful gift. *She could have sold this at the market to buy food,* she thought, *but instead she gave it to me.*

With a smile Majken rose and bowed to her hostesses. As she left the little hut, she was surprised to see the sun was setting. Small wonder she was so stiff. As she walked to her station wagon, she tried to explain to the villagers that if anyone was sick they should tell her right away so that she could bring them medicine. It was difficult to know if they understood.

The next day another oasis, and another visit in an effort to win their confidence. As she left, winding her way through the sand and straining to see the rocks that marked the road, she noticed a group of laborers. She slowed the car, and one of the men came running over to her. With many gestures he asked her to join them. With a quick prayer Majken followed the man to the circle of workers. She sat with them and they passed her a drinking vessel made from the intestine of a goat. Majken was thirsty and responded to their generosity. She marveled at how friendly they were. She felt no danger, only love, as she sat with these strangers beside a desert road.

On impulse she went to the car and brought out two tins of canned beef. They too were passed around the circle, and each of the men took a portion with much lipsmacking and a few belches of gratitude.

Finally Majken pointed up at the sun to indicate that she must leave. They understood and followed her to the car. Everyone was smiling, all traces of restraint gone. The fellowship had been as good as Majken had often enjoyed at the table of lifelong friends.

As she drove back Majken knew that the Lord was preparing these people. The seed was being planted; the harvest would come later. Right now, little by little, day by day, she could see the desert come to life, but what was more important, she had inner assurance that someday they would be able to minister the Bread of Life, which satisfied forever, to these Muslim people.

There were still many places that Majken needed to visit, but the faithful station wagon had other ideas. Pastor Schreiber spent hours in the hot sun, trying to make the "dear old lady" as it was affectionately called, respond. But at last it was agreed that she should be honorably retired.

The new "vehicle" that Majken secured for her visits had advantages and disadvantages quite distinct from the station wagon. There was no problem with gas or rivers and no more flat tires or being stuck in the sand. However, the speed was limited to one mule power. The cost: forty dollars.

Majken noticed on her first trek that the people were even more responsive to her visit. They seemed to be better able to relate to someone who rode a mule than to one who drove a car.

Day after day, Majken climbed aboard her mule and made her rounds. She carried medicine to care for open wounds and simple sores. There did not seem to be as much response now from the people to come to her. She knew that it would be impossible for her to continue to travel at this pace and yet minister to all those who needed it.

Christine encouraged her in her child-like way. She did not understand all that her mother was thinking. She knew only that mother's legs ached, and her back felt like it was going to break in two. *If donkeys only had springs*, thought Majken as she slid into her sleeping bag, looking forward to a good night's sleep.

"*Taala, taala,*" came the cry. Majken sat up and again she heard the words, "*Taala, taala*—come, come." Majken quickly got up, wrapped a blanket around her, and opened the flap of her tent. There stood a man whom she did not recognize, carrying a small gas lantern. He was motioning to Majken to come with him. Majken indicated that she would be right there and went back into her tent. Hurriedly she changed clothes, grabbed her medical bag, leaned over and kissed Christine. The child awakened for a moment, smiled, and went back to sleep. Majken did not know how long she would be gone, but Pastor Schreiber was in a tent nearby and would take care of Christine when she awakened.

Majken climbed on her mule and followed the man. An hour later, they arrived at a hut that she had visited some time before. The man hurried her inside. A woman was lying on the floor, moaning. She held up her arm. Majken could see that she had been stung by a scorpion. Immediately Majken made a tourniquet to block the further flow of blood. She then took a scalpel and made an incision over the place where the scorpion had stung. The patient's arm began to bleed. She sat by the woman until her fear subsided and she fell asleep. By all medical rules the woman should have died. A scorpion bite must be treated immediately, or it is fatal. She felt the woman's forehead. The fever had left. Quietly she slipped out of the hut. The sun was beginning to rise as she looked up and thanked the Lord for His healing. Majken knew that the people would credit her for the healing, but soon enough it would be evident that it was the work of the Great Physician.

It was the breakthrough for which Majken had prayed. The people began coming to her in greater numbers.

"Look at my foot. Me Zineb." Majken recognized a woman from one of the homes she had visited. Zineb exposed her foot, terribly swollen and bluish in color.

"It is possible to save the foot," Majken told her, and then took a scalpel and made a large incision. Other patients stared as the pus gushed out onto the sand. Zineb was very brave. She ground her teeth but did not utter a sound. During the weeks that followed, Zineb returned often to have the wound cared for. No longer was it necessary for her to be carried on the back of her husband, for now she could walk.

A mother came with her seven-year-old daughter. The girl had put her face into a stream to drink and a leech had fastened itself to the inside of her throat. She was having difficulty breathing. The ailment was common among both children and adults.

Majken heated some water and mixed it with salt. The little girl drank the water, vomited, and then drank again. Finally, she took a deep breath. The leech had let go. Majken could only hope that enough salt followed it into the stomach to kill it.

Majken learned some words quicker than others. *"Taala, taala*—come, come" was used almost every day by a desperate mother or father.

Another word heard often was *"hanish*—snake." For some, Majken could administer first aid in time to save their lives; for others, it was too late. Little four-year-old Zoer thought the viper was a stick. She grabbed it, and it bit her. By the time they got her to Majken's tent she was unconscious. Zoer died as Majken was making the incision.

A young man drinking from a stream was bitten on the lip. Within three hours he, too, was dead.

The cry "*taala, taala*" began early in the morning outside her tent flap.

"Can you help me? My wife . . ."

Majken rode her mule for almost two hours. This patient was a naked baby on a dirt floor. The mother was nearby, coughing and short of breath. One look and Majken could tell she had tuberculosis. Her fever and pulse were very high, and she needed hospital care. The closest facility was over ten hours away. Majken knew she would die on the way. It was a pitiful sight watching her trying to feed the infant from her breast. Majken did what she could and headed back to her tent, weeping silently.

Each day she looked with thanksgiving at the walls going up for the clinic. She longed for the day when she could nurse people back to health and care for them in the proper facilities.

Majken was becoming known. Some began calling her "Madam America." She grew to love those whom she met, and they reciprocated. As she continued to gain the confidence of the people, Pastor Schreiber, with Hamid at his side, continued to dig for water and to build houses. The cement had to be hauled in from three hundred miles away, the sand from a river bottom five miles away, and the water in barrels for five miles. It was a slow process.

This was not like Eckernförde in other ways as well. Neither Majken nor Pastor Schreiber were allowed to witness overtly. They dared not even consider building a chapel. However, they did feel the need for some place to worship together. Hamid had been at work among his people, and several had come to know the Lord.

The officials, including the governor, watched with keen

interest the progress at the oasis. They realized the need for a place to worship God, but it would have been an insult to Mohammed to have a visible church. At forty feet down water still had not been found, so there was no objection when the men proceeded to carve out a room eight by ten and five feet high. They had a chapel thirty feet below the ground, where Hamid and his brethren could freely sing, pray, and worship by candlelight as they continued to dig deeper for water.

# 24

# TIME OUT!

The pressures and the lack of proper food began to take their toll. One day Majken collapsed in the middle of the day for "just a short rest." Several hours later, Christine awakened her, telling her that she had been talking incoherently in her sleep.

Her body felt like the hot sand outside. She forced herself out of bed, prepared a syringe of penicillin, and gave herself an injection.

Herr Schreiber came at Christine's urging. He talked of putting her in the VW and moving her to a hospital.

"No," argued Majken, "this is all the medical care these people have. This is all I need."

For several days, Christine prepared their meals and Majken continued to battle the infection. She gave herself several more injections. She knew that people outside the tent each morning were gathered for medical help. "Dear Lord, I must get well," she prayed. "Those people need my help . . . and I need Your help."

Her fever finally broke and Majken knew that the worst was over. As she lay in the hot tent, soaked in perspiration, she thought of the joy and gratefulness that had shone in the eyes of the desert people when they saw how the medicine took effect and they returned to health. Now it was her turn. She was reminded anew that she was only there to give medicine and encouragement. It was God who was doing the healing.

"I am only a servant, and not a very good one," she said aloud. She thought of words she had known all of her life, "Blessed are they which do hunger and thirst after righteousness." She had never understood the significance so plainly as she did now. She knew a little about hunger—she had often fasted and prayed—but she had always had water. Now, living in the Sahara, she could better understand the importance of what Christ was telling His disciples.

Majken realized that she had been so involved in the work that she had forgotten something much more important. She had not been partaking of the Living Water, the fellowship that the Holy Spirit gives to those who spend time with Him. The work was not unimportant; rather it was so important that it was necessary that she be set aside so that she could be taught to do it right. She had come dangerously close to changing true vision into nothing more than a social gospel, a great work lacking power. She wondered how many people in the past had come to such a desert in their lives and had dried up and withered away without producing any fruit. She vowed to never let it happen to her again.

Majken spent much of her recuperation writing to those who had long supported her in prayer and giving. Recovery was slow, and finally it was necessary for Majken to return to Germany. This coincided with the dedication of the new clinic-dormitory. She looked forward to the event with great anticipation, but it proved to be a subdued homecoming. Sister Ruth broke the news.

"Sister Ella had not been feeling well. We took her to the hospital, and she seemed to be making a good recovery. She was told she could return to the home after a few days' rest. Then early Wednesday morning we received the call. We were all stunned. A blood clot had formed in her leg and traveled to her heart. She went to sleep and never woke up."

Majken found it difficult to believe. Sister Ella, the mother to all the girls, the one who had taught her how to take care of little Christine—Sister Ella was gone.

There was no need to discuss a memorial. The evidence of Sister Ella's work was alive throughout Germany. While others might build with bricks and stone, Sister Ella had built new lives with love, prayer, and compassion.

Majken had always emphasized that work with marble would fall to pieces. Work with metal would rust. Even homes would one day crumble and fall. But to work with the souls of children and build the right foundation with the Word of God, "in such hearts is engraved," said Majken, "something that will endure forever."

It was time to reestablish her ties in America. After a brief stop in Sweden it was on to the States and Cousin Joseph's home outside Chicago. While there, she received a call from Mrs. Ray Brown in Galesburg, Illinois.

"Majken, the local fellowship of the National Association of Christian Churches is having a fellowship meeting here in our church," she explained excitedly. "We would like you to attend."

Majken and Christine went to the meeting and told of the new work in Morocco. When the meeting was over, Majken was taken outside. Sitting in front of the church was a brand-new Jeep Land Rover, just the kind of vehicle needed for the desert. Painted on both sides of the hood in red, white, and blue, were the words, "Madam America."

Majken had not been back to the United States in three years. There were many requests for meetings with different churches. As was always the case, it was necessary to remind the people of the work of Mission Kinderheim. And now the story of the new work in Morocco needed to be told.

With Christine at her side, Majken made another cross-country trip, this time in her bright new Jeep. Never before had she appreciated so much the modern motels and paved highways. She vowed that she would never again take the United States for granted. Yet all the while she traveled she felt an urgency to return to the Sahara.

Pastor Schreiber had written to say that the sand was getting damp at two hundred fifty feet. They would soon have fresh water. He added that the roof was now on the clinic and the sick were still coming to Majken's tent daily, in hopes that she had returned.

Several weeks later, the Jeep was placed aboard a ship bound for Europe. Gifts from the churches for the home in Eckernförde and materials for the clinic in Morocco were carefully packed and shipped to Tangier. Majken and Christine flew ahead to Germany.

Majken was overwhelmed at the supplies that had been collected. There were examining tables, wheelchairs, medicines, and almost all the equipment needed to supply a modern dispensary, including beds, linens, and blankets.

February 15, 1972. On that beautiful, clear morning, nine years after their first trip to the Sahara, Majken, Pastor Schreiber, Hamid, and several faithful prayer warriors from Scandinavia—Pastors Moen, Schelbeck, and Manna—stood together as they dedicated what was then the only such clinic in the Sahara. The many Moroccans who had been brought back from ill health joined in the ceremony. Some bowed their heads—they had labored day after day in their long search for water, which was now flowing through shiny pipes to the surface, past the underground chapel. In the process some had found something more precious: Living Water.

# 25

## "... AND ALL THESE THINGS"

Within two years the desert began to bloom. There were corn, potatoes, watermelon, and alfalfa. An almond grove flourished.

Crowds continued to gather each day at the clinic; but because of trouble on the Algerian border foreigners were warned that they might soon be forced to leave. Majken began immediately to train helpers. After treating her patients in the early morning cool, Majken toiled long hours in the afternoon heat, teaching three young men how to bathe wounds, make incisions with a scalpel, and suture. They learned quickly, and in a short time Majken was moving deeper into the desert to reach those who had not yet been helped. Christine, as always, was her constant companion and helper.

The new Jeep took them places where they could never go before. But still there were times when Majken knew only the hand of the Lord had rescued them. Returning to the clinic late one evening, the Jeep got stuck in the sand. Majken and Christine had to walk for four hours before they found help. They prayed for protection from the night predators which were about. It took four men and five hours of hard work before they could dig the Jeep out.

The terrain was so treacherous in some areas that Majken

was warned not to go, but there were people out there who needed help. There were areas where Jeeps could not pass and donkeys became exhausted, so a camel was obtained. It became a common sight: Majken astride Gustav Vasa, the King of the Desert, heading for some isolated oasis with her bag of medicine.

Inevitably, the word came. The border conflicts had increased and all foreigners were ordered out of the desert.

Majken and Christine, the last to leave, bid a sad farewell to the oasis. Their regret was tempered with praise at what the Lord had done. They took one last look at the terrain. Once it had been nothing but rocks. Now lush watermelons and other garden products dotted the landscape. Several miles of pipeline fed water to the thirsty roots, keeping them fertile and productive. Six families occupied the houses that had been built, brick by brick, in the hot desert sun. The clinic was now the focal point of the entire province.

Children had been taught how to build homes, how to dig wells, how to nurture food from the ground.

Majken saved her final good-bye for one of the greatest prizes of the desert: Hamid. He now drank deeply of the Living Water, as did his wife, and the two children that Majken had delivered.

Where snakes once slithered at will, water moved quietly down a cement trench. Through the tears, Majken saw a desert blooming. As the Jeep turned and headed down the road, she waved farewell to the fruit of their labors.

# 26

## "FIFI," HONDURAS, AND NEW HOPE

Majken was enjoying the comforts of her little room in Eckernförde. Her body was being given an opportunity to rebuild itself after living in the desert for the better part of nine years. As was her practice, she always kept up on international events, reading the major magazines and daily newspapers.

It was September 19, 1974. She had just finished eating breakfast with the children in the dining room when her eyes froze on a headline: "Hurricane devastates Honduras." Tears welled up in her eyes as she read the article. "6,000 people dead; 538,480 homeless; crops destroyed; 100,000 dairy cattle destroyed."

Majken put the paper down and began to pray. She had no idea where Honduras was, other than it was somewhere in South America. She visualized the children and heard their cries for help. They needed food and clothing. Many were, no doubt, orphaned.

"Lord, what can I do?"

After praying she went to the library and started to read about this country that suddenly had been catapulted into her life.

Honduras, the second largest Central American country, is bordered by Guatemala on one side, El Salvador and Nicaragua on

171

the other, and the Caribbean on the north. Of the 1,188,765 people, 70 percent make their living farming.

As she read, studied, and prayed, she could see that there was plenty to do in Honduras, even without a hurricane.

Then she began to protest. "But, Lord, what can I do? Our finances are already strained with the work here at Eckernförde and Morocco."

Majken sought the counsel of the Sisters and other members of the Board. All agreed that there were many needs in Honduras, but there were needs all over the world. Besides, Majken was the only one there who really knew where the country was located.

"How many here knew about the Sahara, until we went there?" Majken challenged in return.

"But, Majken, you are still weak," her friends reminded her. "You need more time to regain your health. And don't forget you have a little daughter in school."

Majken had a few thoughts of her own. She knew that she was weak, but the Lord had always given her strength when she needed it. And she could not possibly be as weak as the victims of Hurricane "Fifi." At least she had shelter, clothes, and good food to eat.

"Lord, should we start a new work now? Should we take on this added responsibility?" Once again she laid herself before the Lord.

The answer was yes.

One month later Majken and Christine boarded a plane for a city that a short time ago they had never heard of: San Pedro Sula. The city of 58,600 was located in the northern part of Honduras. They stepped off the plane with only an address of a local Swedish mission.

Part of the annual rainfall—normally 100 inches—had just fallen. Steam rose from the pavement, and they dodged large puddles of water in their walk to the terminal. On the street they found a taxi driver who understood the universal language: American dollars, which would take them to a good hotel in the city. Christine made a game out of trying to guess how old the the taxi was. They settled on somewhere close to Majken's own age. The roads were full of potholes, but the scenery was even more jarring. Flimsy shacks seemed to stretch for blocks. The people looked much like those in the Sahara, except their faces were flatter. Everyone had black hair. The expressions of the children were the same all over the world. Some waved to them as they drove along.

They had to detour several times. Many bridges were out. It appeared that little had been done to restore roads, homes, and anything else damaged by Fifi.

They checked into a hotel reserved for foreign visitors. After changing into clothes better adapted to the heat and humidity, Majken purchased a map of the country. Tomorrow they would rent a car and travel to some of the outlying areas. Majken wanted to see for herself where the needs were. She still did not know what she was to do or where she was to go.

After a good night's rest and the first of many breakfasts of rice and beans, Majken pulled out her map and began to drive. Not all of the highways were open. Even in the best of times, the roads apparently were not very good. She noticed on the map the notation that Honduras was the only Central American nation not touched by the Pan American Highway, the strip of paved roads that runs uninterrupted from the top of Alaska to the furthermost tip of South America.

It was not necessary to drive far to find evidence of the enormous number of children needing food. It was only a matter of where and how.

Away from the city, the poverty was even more obvious. There were entire encampments of people living in as severe a state of squalor as Majken had ever witnessed. The heat added a stifling dimension. The people seemed to be inert. The distended stomachs of the children indicated severe malnutrition.

Majken wondered what the conditions had been like before Fifi. Had it always been this terrible?

Back at the hotel, Majken and Christine fell on their beds, exhausted. Christine fell asleep almost immediately, but Majken continued to review what she had seen. Over and over again she asked herself, *What can we do?*

What was it that the people needed? The question, "Why haven't they rebuilt more?" kept coming back to her. Were they all sick? Was the malnutrition so severe that they did not have the energy?

It was a question that she did not dwell on very long. She thought about what a mission could accomplish immediately. She saw in her mind's eye the hungry children and mentally began to design a feeding program. They would need a building for storage and distribution. And rice and milk would be top priority.

Just thinking about the logistics caused her to place her hands over her eyes and pray. The venture was far too big for mere man to contemplate, let alone for a woman and a child to undertake.

The next day they drove to the small city of La Lima where the Swedish mission station was located. They were enthusiastically welcomed by Hans and Stine Alsbo. The Alsbos had been in Honduras for fourteen years and were scheduled to return to Sweden shortly. Majken made it clear that she did not want to duplicate what had already been accomplished but desired to help in any way that she could. If this meant supporting an existing work, then she would be happy to do so.

After several hours, she had a deeper understanding of the problems. She was correct in her observation that little

174

rebuilding had been done since Fifi. The reason was that the country was so poor. The storm had destroyed much of their crops. Food was very scarce. Many villages had been totally destroyed and the people never went back to the ruins. They simply moved to higher ground, and when the water receded, they found pieces of wood, cardboard, and old rags, and started another village to replace the one destroyed. Majken was assured that almost any plans could only help the situation in Honduras.

As she was about to leave, a group of Honduran women came to the door. Hans talked to them for a few moments.

"Here is a perfect example of what I was telling you," he said. "We have delegations like this coming to us every day. They are from a new village of about five thousand not far from here. It is called New Hope. They come asking for medicine, food—anything that we can give them." Hans shrugged his shoulders. "We will do what we can, but so much is needed."

Now no one needed to tell Majken what to do. She felt it from the tip of her toes to the top of her head. The words "New Hope" went through her like an electric charge.

"Maybe that is where we can begin," she told Hans. "May I visit the village?"

With Hans as navigator they set out for New Hope. It was difficult to tell where one refugee village ended and another started. They drove for several miles away from the city. People sat in the dust alongside the road, but there was no other activity. Just ahead, through the glare of the sun, Majken could see a large cluster of shacks.

"There it is," said Hans. "We will have to walk now. The road ends here."

They got out of the car and made their way toward the settlement. As they came closer, Majken witnessed the scenery of the day before: the ramshackle huts, the distended stomachs, people dressed in rags.

175

"New Hope," said Majken. "Hardly an appropriate name, is it?"

"They used to have a nice, quiet village of ten thousand," Hans replied. "They were poor, but at least they had wooden homes and a few chickens and pigs. Half their number died in the storm. Everyone here has lost a father, mother, or a child. I think they are still in a state of shock. But they want a new village, a new beginning. That is why they call it New Hope.

"There are no schools here, and no work for the men. Many children die each month because of disease and malnutrition. Water is scarce."

"How can they live without water?" asked Majken. She had spent enough time in the Sahara to understand the importance of a good water supply. "Don't they have a well?"

"Yes," said Hans, "there it is right up ahead. Let's take a look at it."

Just ahead was a large group of people gathered in a circle. They stepped aside and made way for Hans, Majken, and Christine. Majken could not believe what she saw. A small gasoline engine was drawing water from the well, but it was only a trickle. People came and waited to fill whatever container they could produce.

Before Majken could say anything, Hans explained that there was actually plenty of water in the well, but they did not have a pump. They had had one, but they could not pay for it, so the company came and took it away.

"You mean they would not let these people keep a pump for water just because they could not pay for it?" asked Majken in disbelief.

"The people in town have to live, too. If they gave a pump to every village that needed one, they would go broke."

Majken's disbelief turned to anger. She thought of how the Moroccans had dug the well in the desert and how the

176

water made a desert bloom. And here, in a land that was supposed to be civilized, because there was no money, the people were drinking water from stagnant pools.

"No wonder these people are sick," said Majken.

Hans supplied an interpreter for Majken so that she could return to the village several more times. As was her policy, she visited the local officials to ask for help and obtain permission to work.

She contacted the department of health. They agreed that the people needed water. "But," they said, "we have a half million people homeless. We cannot give all of them pumps for their wells."

Majken knew that she would not get any help, but she did get what she wanted: their moral support. She could now say that she was working with the blessing of the authorities. Majken began to study how to bring them Living Water as well. The work in Honduras was underway.

# 27

# "... IF WE
# FAINT NOT"

Majken soon learned that Hurricane Fifi was the only thing that had moved with much speed in Honduras since Columbus landed there in 1502. The pump was ordered, paid for, and finally delivered. Standing by while the workmen put it together took more patience than Majken could sometimes muster. She could not make them understand that children were dying each day—children who would not die if they had decent water. The workmen from the city weren't terribly impressed with her pleas.

Majken made several trips in the year that followed to the United States to involve her friends in this new ministry. As before, they responded generously, and soon Majken returned to Honduras with new encouragement. She enrolled Christine, now eleven, in school. She spoke no Spanish, so they started her in the second grade and moved her up as she learned the language. Majken also began to study the language. She knew her work was hampered as long as she was at the mercy of an interpreter.

Finally, after several months, the new pump was working. A thousand-gallon water tank was placed on a tower over the well. City officials came from La Lima to see it. They would use it as a model project for other villages.

Majken was still concerned about the spiritual needs of

the people. She wanted a Sunday school for the children. She learned that they could not study religion in the public schools, at least not the kind that Majken wanted taught. They would need to build their own facility, which meant that they would need land. A Sunday school also needed a church and a pastor. But from where?

There were so many people that were physically ill. There would also have to be a clinic.

Day by day the plans came to life, after much diligent prayer. In March, 1976, Majken rented a small house. Eight months later, on a piece of land that had been purchased and which was located right in the heart of the city, Emmanuel Church was dedicated. More than two hundred fifty people filled the wooden benches while several hundred more gathered outside to hear their new pastor—Pastor Jose Majia.

Two blocks away the walls began to go up for the clinic.

What was still missing was something that would help the children get a better education. All students in Honduras were required by law to wear school uniforms. Without a uniform, a child simply forfeited his right to an education, and the majority of the children were in rags. Majken also had a burden for the young mothers who had never had a chance to improve themselves.

With a stroke of ingenuity Majken drew up plans to meet both of these needs. A small room was built on the side of Emmanuel Church to house a sewing school for girls. Majken bought eight sewing machines and enrolled local girls for a nine-month course. When they entered the school, they received a Bible and the promise of daily Bible studies with Pastor Majia.

The first class of twenty-one students made their own uniforms, then they made uniforms free of charge for those children who could not afford them.

With New Hope on its feet, Majken moved on to another

village called "The Twenty-third of September." It was common to name a village after a certain date, the significance of which was often soon forgotten.

This village was as poor as New Hope, with the same malnourished children, hopeless mothers, and unemployed fathers.

Through the generosity of Majken's American friends a cinder block multi-purpose building was built that served as a kitchen, providing one hundred fifty children two meals a day; a kindergarten for local children; and a sewing school. It also housed a Sunday school class of one hundred and a church of regulars.

Majken's concern extended to the countryside. She bought eight hundred fifty dollars' worth of cement to build a bridge so that the people could travel outside of their own village to work and to shop.

Another village had sixty homes without roofs. Majken provided three thousand dollars' worth of roofing material, and the villagers put roofs on their own houses.

While traveling one day, she came across a village by the name of Brisas Delsauce. Fifteen hundred people had moved onto a plot of land after Fifi had rampaged across the country and had built homes. Then it was discovered that they had built on private property, and the landlord was evicting them. None of them had money or a place to go. The government had no welfare programs.

Majken found a piece of available land next to the village of New Hope. A road was bulldozed and the land subdivided into tiny plots. Financing was arranged so that each family could buy the land on credit at the cost of twelve lempiras or six dollars a month for five years.

Majken also provided building materials for the new homes. Again, there was a need to feed the children as well as supply water for the people. Always she was concerned that both the physical and spiritual needs of the people be met.

The Haven of Rest radio broadcast, which had continued to support the Eckernförde ministry, asked for the privilege of raising the money for a well and multi-purpose room for this small village.

Soon the well was dug, topped with a thirty-foot tower and thousand-gallon water tank. The multi-purpose room, equipped with modern kitchen equipment, began almost immediately to feed two hundred children one meal per day. A dedicated group of Christian women supervised the project.

A medical clinic and a special reading school for women soon followed.

Majken never ran out of projects. Another village of six thousand people had only two toilets. Long lines formed outside the facilities from early morning until late at night. Worse than that, the very young and the very old never bothered to stand in line. The situation created severe health problems for everyone in the village. Disease was rampant. Majken bought cement and wood, and the men of the village built one hundred outhouses. The cost was thirty dollars each, a small price for the lives saved from disease.

The mission in Honduras was much more than wells, walls, food lines, clinics, schools, and churches. It was, as in Eckernförde and Morocco, people.

One such person was Martha. In the villages, people often used an open oil drum for a stove. Martha was preparing a meal for herself and her two boys, Servilio, five, and Juan, thirteen, when she had an epileptic seizure and fell against the blazing stove. She was burned horribly. For a long time she lay in the hospital in terrible pain, until infection took her life.

Majken gathered up the two boys and took over the funeral arrangements, including having the girls at the sewing school make a white dress for her burial suit. The boys she placed in the home of a local pastor.

In the midst of all this sorrow and sweat, triumph and

toil, came more heartache. The year 1975 produced one of the worst droughts in the history of Honduras. The crops dried up and many people died. Food lines were never-ending.

But the worst blow fell in November, 1979. The rest of the world was occupied with events in Iran where a group of Americans were being held hostage by radical Muslims. In Honduras, an entire nation was being held hostage. The villain was water.

For days the rains came down, twenty-four hours a day. In La Lima, 10,600 people lost their homes.

In Brisas Delsauce, men cut a hole in the roof of the multi-purpose building to hoist the refrigerator and the clothing to safety. They stayed in boats and guarded the building, waiting for the water to recede.

More bridges were destroyed under the terrific pressure of swollen mountain streams.

A drowning incident in the village "Twenty-third of September" was typical. The high dike had broken and a woman saw her only possessions, a bed, table, and chair, floating away. Without hesitation she jumped into the rushing water after them. She disappeared and four children were left to be cared for.

Finally, in mid-December, the rains stopped, and the water began to recede. Majken and Christine set up soup lines feeding as many as they could. All the money they could raise was used to buy food.

Slowly, a semblance of Honduran normalcy returned. The weather grew cold. Majken bought material, and her students in the sewing school made five hundred blankets.

The water receded at New Hope and the village returned to the everyday problem of keeping alive. One more catastrophe had been survived and they prepared for the next one.

One evening after a particularly frustrating day, Majken

lay on her damp bed. The first time she had come to Honduras, Fifi had torn the land apart. Now it was the floods. But in the meantime, many people had tasted of Living Water. Many more were still waiting. Majken rested her hand over her eyes. She had had little sleep for the past two months, but the villages, the wells, the school survived, and so would she. Quietly the words came from deep inside: "Bear ye one another's burden and so fulfill the law of Christ. And let us not be weary in well doing; for in due season we shall reap if we faint not." She fell asleep. Chapter one of the work in Honduras had been written.

# EPILOGUE

Today, Majken lives in Mission, Texas, on a small piece of land next door to Joseph and Daga Mattson-Boze. Christine is an American citizen and graduates from high school in 1981.

Much of Majken's time is spent visiting the three continents where Mission Kinderheim is engaged in work. Since her vision in Sweden in 1945, many events have taken place in her life. Most of them she modestly passes off with a shrug of her shoulders. She is, for instance, the recipient of the prestigious "Cross of Merit with Ribbon" presented by the Federal Republic of Germany for her work at Eckernförde. She has had many battles with illness, including major surgery for cancer.

There are no computers, no large mailing lists, no pleading for funds in her work, but rather only a quiet, resolute belief that God never creates a need in one person's life without supplying another person who will meet that need.

Mildred Hess, with the help of another faithful worker, Ruth Edsom, runs a small office in Stamford, Connecticut in conjunction with Mission Kinderheim. Majken continues to write personally to those who want to know what they can do.

She adamantly insists that it is not her work. If there is to be any credit given beyond the Lord, she bestows it on the many nameless people who have been urged by God to respond and in obedience have done so. Her vision remains clear: She is little more than the arms and hands of Jesus, reaching out to transfer a blessing from one person to another: from a farm in Canada to a refugee camp in Germany; from a widow's home in Sweden to a kitchen full of food in Eckernförde; from a modest home in Florida to a snake-infested desert in Morocco; from a church in Connecticut to a disease-ridden village in Honduras.

In the early days of the work at Eckernförde, Majken was perplexed over one young boy who, though in obvious need of all the nutrition he could absorb, always left a portion of his food on the plate. "Why," asked Majken, "do you leave food? Why don't you eat it all?" Meals passed, and the boy did not reply. Finally in exasperation he blurted out, "If I eat it all now, there will not be any food left for the next meal."

Thankfully, today, there is plenty of food for the one hundred thirty-five children at Eckernförde. But the need for spiritual food is still great. Communism, whose vast armies and inflexible leadership destroys a nation beginning at the top, creates a certain kind of refugee who is now cared for by the West German government.

But another kind of refugee has emerged out of this highly industrialized nation. They are the victims of materialism. The devastation is from the bottom up; the disease is destroying nations, one family at a time. It is this kind of refugee who now is being cared for at Eckernförde. Some stay several months; others several years. The hunger for acceptance and love is as real in these young men and women as was the physical hunger experienced thirty years ago.

In an effort to minister more aptly at Eckernförde, land has been purchased in an isolated area ten miles from the present home. There homes will be built for young couples whose marriages are about to collapse. They will live together under the close supervision of Spirit-filled workers for periods of one month to a year, as they work out their problems. Men and women who have already been divorced will also be invited to stay at the home, to take the time to allow God to heal their inner hurts.

Most appropriately, the Sisters at Eckernförde still wear the pins with the motto, "Pray and work."

In Morocco, the oasis now named BouRbia Two continues to thrive. Instead of traveling sixty miles for water, the local people now come to BourRbia Two and drink from four wells.

The clinic continues to minister each day. The entire village, including the clinic, is staffed by local people under the direction of Hamid. After a training stint at Eckernförde, he is considered an expert in irrigation, construction, medicine, and "that foreign religion."

The village is self-supporting, except for the diesel fuel that draws the water out of the wells and some of the salaries for several leaders. This continues to be the responsibility of Mission Kinderheim. There is still one project not yet completed: a school for the children. It is a need that was dramatically emphasized in a recent report from BouRbia Two.

> The sun was burning . . . sandstorms howled over the homes, and the people waited for rain. Dark clouds gathered over the Atlas Mountains. The horizon turned yellow. But the children had to continue their education. Their school was a three-mile walk, but they could take a shortcut through the dry river bottom. This day was no different. The children walked happily, chattering, stopping now and then to throw a stone, and did not hear the rumble behind them. No one knows for sure if the children ever heard the approaching avalanche of water from the sudden cloudburst in the mountains. It took several days to find the bodies of the five missing children. Two boys, the only sons of a proud father, were found three days later, miles

downstream. Today, two suits of clothes, filled with sand and clay, lay in a home as mute testimony to the need for a school. One of the boys was Hamid's son whom Majken helped welcome into the world. The men have cut off their beards as a sign of deepest mourning.

The sorrow over the drownings was deep, but even yet there are signs of new life at BouRbia Two. The children, like the wells and the clinic, represent seed planted in the desert, waiting to sprout and bloom, producing fruit fit for the Master's service.

Then there is Honduras. The story of the son of Martha, the woman who fell on the oil drum stove and died of the burns, tells it best. After she was buried, her two sons were taken to the mission at New Hope to be cared for. Juan, the oldest, was grief-stricken. He attended services at Emmanuel Church but never communicated with anyone. He finally met friends who took him to the slums, where he fell into deep trouble and was not heard of for several months. One day a message was received at the church. The boy had broken his arm when he fell off a tractor. Gangrene set in and his arm had to be amputated. Majken found him in a hospital near death. He was moved to a better facility, and after many blood transfusions his condition improved.

After two further operations and skin grafts to prepare the way for an artificial limb, the boy was asked, "What about your future? What can we do?"

He looked at Majken and said, "Without help, I do not have a future."

Today, he lives in the home of a pastor and has found new hope.

This boy in Honduras is one of nearly seventeen thousand that Mission Kinderheim has helped. But there are thousands more who are in situations as desperate as this young man. They have no hope and no future unless someone reaches out to care for them.

## MAJKEN

At sixty-four, Majken still sees the vision—wide streets, people with hopeless looks of despair, wringing hands, and empty, haunting eyes. She hears the cry, "Will you help us?" Her answer is still, "Yes, Lord."